A2 Music
Study Guide

Edexcel

Paul Terry and
David Bowman

**R· RHINEGOLD
EDUCATION**

www.rhinegoldeducation.co.uk

Music Study Guides

GCSE, AS and A2 Music Study Guides (AQA, Edexcel and OCR)
GCSE, AS and A2 Music Listening Tests (AQA, Edexcel and OCR)
GCSE, AS and A2 Music Revision Guides (AQA, Edexcel and OCR)
AS/A2 Music Technology Study Guide (Edexcel)
AS/A2 Music Technology Listening Tests (Edexcel)
AS/A2 Music Technology Revision Guides (Edexcel)

Also available from Rhinegold Education

Key Stage 3 Listening Tests: Book 1 and Book 2
AS and A2 Music Harmony Workbooks
GCSE and AS Music Composition Workbooks
GCSE and AS Music Literacy Workbooks
Dictionary of Music in Sound
Understanding Popular Music
Music Technology from Scratch
Musicals in Focus, Baroque Music in Focus, Film Music in Focus

First published 2012 in Great Britain by
Rhinegold Education
14-15 Berners Street
London W1T 3LJ, UK
www.rhinegoldeducation.co.uk

© 2012 Rhinegold Education
a division of Music Sales Limited

You should always check the current requirements of the examination, since these may change.
Copies of the Edexcel specification can be downloaded from the Edexcel website at www.edexcel.com
Edexcel Publications telephone: 01623 467467, fax: 01623 450481,
email: publication.orders@edexcel.com

Edexcel A2 Music Study Guide 4th edition
Order No. RHG302
ISBN: 978-1-78038-494-8

Exclusive Distributors:
Music Sales Ltd
Distribution Centre, Newmarket Road, Bury St Edmunds,
Suffolk IP33 3YB, UK

Printed in the EU

Contents

Introduction . . . . *page* 5

Unit 4: Extended Performance 7

Unit 5: Composition and Technical Study 13

Unit 6: Further Musical Understanding 30

        Set works for examination in 2013

                Instrumental music 35

                Applied music 62

        Set works for examination in 2014

                Instrumental music 79

                Applied music 106

Glossary 122

Elements of Music 132

Index of Works 136

The authors

David Bowman and Paul Terry have co-authored many books in support of A-level music, including study guides for Rhinegold Publishing and the books *Aural Matters*, *Aural Matters in Practice* and *Listening Matters* published by Schott.

Paul Terry has taught music from primary to postgraduate level. He was a music examiner for nearly 30 years and has worked as a consultant for several examination boards. He also served as a member of the Secondary Examinations Council and its successor the Schools Examinations and Assessment Council. He was chief examiner for the Oxford and Cambridge Schools Examinations Board (now part of OCR) and he was a chief examiner for London Examinations (now part of Edexcel). In addition to the books listed above, Paul has written *Musicals in Focus* for Rhinegold Publishing and is co-author with William Lloyd of *Music in Sequence*, *Classics in Sequence*, *Rock in Sequence*, and *Rehearse, Direct and Play*, published by Musonix Publishing.

David Bowman was for 20 years director of music at Ampleforth College and was a chief examiner for the University of London Schools Examination Board (now Edexcel) from 1982 to 1998. He now spends more time with his family, horses and dogs. In addition to the titles listed above, David's publications include the *London Anthology of Music* (University of London Schools Examinations Board), *Sound Matters* (co-authored with Bruce Cole, published by Schott), *Analysis Matters* (two volumes, published by Rhinegold) and many analytical articles for *Music Teacher*. He is a contributor to the *Collins Classical Music Encyclopedia*, edited by Stanley Sadie, and is the author of the *Rhinegold Dictionary of Music in Sound*.

Acknowledgements

The authors would like to thank Dr Hugh Benham for his comments on the opening chapters of this book, and the Rhinegold team of Katharine Allenby, Elisabeth Boulton and Christina Forde. We are also grateful to the following for permission to use printed excerpts from their publications:

Francis Poulenc: Sonata for Horn, Trumpet and Trombone © Copyright 1924 Chester Music Ltd. All Rights Reserved. International Copyright Secured.

Steve Reich: *New York Counterpoint* © Copyright 1986 by Hendon Music Inc., a Boosey & Hawkes company. Reproduced by permission of Boosey & Hawkes Music Publishers Ltd.

Leonard Bernstein: *On the Waterfront* © Copyright 1955, 1962 by Amberson Holdings LLC, LBMPC, Publisher. Boosey & Hawkes, Inc., an Imagem Company. Sole Print Licensee. International copyright secured. All rights reserved. Reproduced by permission of Boosey & Hawkes Music Publishers Ltd.

Planet of the Apes: music by Jerry Goldsmith © Copyright 1968 Warner-Tamerlane Publishing Co., USA. Warner/Chappell North America Limited. All Rights Reserved. International Copyright Secured.

Black and Tan Fantasy: Words & Music by Edward Ellington & James Miley © Copyright 1927 (Renewed 1954) Gotham Music Service Incorporated. EMI Music Publishing Limited. All Rights Reserved. International Copyright Secured.

Anton Webern: Quartet Op.22 © Copyright 1932 Universal Edition A. G., Wien. All Rights Reserved. International Copyright Secured.

'Take her to sea, Mr Murdoch' from *Titanic*, music by James Horner © Copyright 1998 TCF Music Publishing Incorporated/Fox Film Music Corporation/Twentieth Century Fox Incorporated, USA. Hal Leonard Corporation. All Rights Reserved. International Copyright Secured.

Introduction

Course overview

A-level Music consists of six units. The first three make up the AS exam while units 4–6 form the A2 exam.

Unit 4: Extended Performance

This unit accounts for 30% of the marks for A2 Music. You will have to perform a balanced programme of pieces of your choice lasting between 12 and 15 minutes. Any instrument (or voice) can be used, and you may perform as a soloist and/or with a small ensemble. Your programme can be presented at any time before the end of the course, but it must consist of a single performance – you are not allowed to assemble a portfolio of pieces presented on different occasions. However, you can repeat the entire programme (although not individual pieces from it) on another occasion if you and your teacher are not happy with your first attempt. Your programme will be recorded and marked by your teacher, and the recording will be sent to an Edexcel examiner who will check the mark that you have been awarded.

Unit 5: Composition and Technical Study

This unit also accounts for 30% of the marks for A2 Music and is based on a choice of briefs that will be set by Edexcel at the start of your course. You have to complete two tasks under controlled conditions: two compositions, or two technical studies, or one of each. The work is then recorded, and scores and recordings sent to an Edexcel examiner for marking.

Unit 6: Further Musical Understanding

This unit accounts for 40% of the marks for A2 Music. You will study two groups of set works, as well as techniques for answering questions on unfamiliar music. At the end of the course you will sit a two-hour exam paper in three sections:

➢ In Section A you will have to answer questions on recordings of music that will be unfamiliar, although the excerpts played will be related to the set works you have studied

➢ In Section B you will have to answer two questions on one of the groups of set works

➢ In Section C you will have to answer an essay question about three pieces from the other group of set works.

You will be allowed to refer to an unmarked copy of NAM throughout the exam. Your answers to this paper will be sent to an Edexcel examiner for marking.

The set works change each year and are not the same as those you studied for AS Music. They are all taken from the *New Anthology of Music*, referred to as NAM in the rest of this book.

NAM is published by Peters Edition Ltd, ISBN 978-1-901507-03-4 (with a set of four CDs, ISBN 978-1-901507-04-1), and is available from Edexcel publications (see page 2) or from any music retailer.

Getting started

This book will help you prepare for the exam by providing tips and advice for performing and composing, along with detailed notes on the set works that you will need to study. Explanations of technical terms printed in bold type can be found in the glossary at the end of the book. If you need further help with these, or with other terminology you encounter during the course, we recommend that you consult the *Rhinegold Dictionary of Music in Sound* by David Bowman. This resource not only gives detailed explanations of a wide range of musical concepts, but also illustrates them using a large number of specially recorded examples on CD, enabling you to hear directly how theory relates to the actual sounds of music.

As with AS Music, you will have little more than 24 weeks in which to complete your composing and performing coursework, and to prepare for Unit 6, so it is essential to be well-organised from day one of the course.

Planning is the secret of success. Choosing music and beginning practice for performing need to get under way as soon as possible, as does preparation for Unit 5. Work for Unit 6 needs to continue throughout the course and be completed in time to allow for revision and the working of several mock papers in the weeks before the actual exam.

Take responsibility for your own progress, using this book as a starting point for your studies, and remember that by meeting deadlines you can avoid the stress of a huge workload in the final weeks of the course.

It is worth repeating the advice we gave in our AS Music Study Guide, because it applies equally to A2 Music.

Firstly, it will help enormously if you try to spot connections between the music you hear, the music you play and the music you compose. Understanding the context and structure of music will increase your enjoyment when listening, inform your performing and illuminate your composing. Composing, performing, listening and understanding are all related aspects of the study of music, and this integration of activities is an important aspect of the course you are taking.

Secondly, try to broaden your musical experience by learning new pieces, taking part in group activities, improvising on your instrument to create different moods and new sounds, and listening to as wide a range of music as you can, both recorded and live. Don't just listen to comfortably familiar music – look for opportunities to broaden your understanding of new types and styles of music by listening to broadcasts and tracks available on the internet, and by going to concerts. This will help to increase your musical understanding and build your confidence as a musician. It should also help to make your year of studying A2 Music highly enjoyable.

Good luck!

The *Rhinegold Dictionary of Music in Sound* by David Bowman is published by Rhinegold Education, ISBN 978-0946890-87-3.

Unit 4: Extended Performance

What, when and where

You are required to give a performance that lasts between 12 and 15 minutes. It doesn't matter if you run a little over this limit, but if the total playing time is less than 12 minutes your mark will be reduced.

Your entire programme must be performed in a single continuous session – you are not allowed to assemble a recording of pieces given on different occasions. If you are not satisfied with your performance, you are allowed to repeat it on a later occasion, but you must present the complete programme again – you cannot repeat just selected items.

You may perform on any instrument (including singing). You can include pieces played on different instruments if you wish, but there is no advantage in doing so. It is best avoided unless you really do play two instruments to an equally good standard.

> Throughout this chapter the word 'instrument' includes the voice.

You can perform as a soloist (with accompaniment, if appropriate) and/or as a member of a group of up to five performers. Any style of music is acceptable, but read the notes about 'difficulty level' on the next page.

Your performance can take place in class, or as part of a concert either within your school or in the wider community. Your teacher will advise what is the best type of occasion for you. It can take place at any time during the course until the date when marks have to be sent to Edexcel (usually about the middle of May). Again, your teacher will advise on a suitable date.

It is a good idea to have several practice runs at formal performance during the course. Performing for at least 12 minutes is demanding for all musicians, especially wind players and singers, and the added strain of being recorded and assessed will almost certainly make you a little tense. You will be far less anxious if you have experienced performing the full programme to others before the actual assessment day.

Remember that the final assessment should not be left until the end of the course – you will be busy revising and completing coursework for all your subjects by then, and will have little time in which to focus on doing your best in performing. Choose a date with your teacher that is early enough to allow time for at least one later performance in case you should be unwell or not ready for the planned occasion.

Choosing a programme

Plan your programme carefully. It should be well-balanced, with variety of style, mood and tempo. Playing a succession of similar slow movements, for example, would not be a good idea.

You can present a single substantial work providing that it lasts for at least 12 minutes and includes sufficient variety within itself. However, most people present a group of shorter pieces. If you wish, these could be linked by a common theme, such as:

➤ A set of dance movements in different styles

➤ Songs by different composers that are all settings of words by Shakespeare

➤ A group of jazz standards played in contrasting styles.

A good way to achieve contrast is to perform music from several different periods (such as Baroque, Classical, Romantic and Modern) or in several different styles (such as covers of popular songs from four different decades). If your pieces all come from the same stylistic period, it is particularly important that they are varied in tempo and character.

Choosing the right music for your programme is very important. You are not allowed to include pieces that you played for the AS performing unit, but other works that you know well are likely to be a better choice than pieces that you are currently in the process of learning (unless you are really sure that you will have totally mastered them well before the assessment).

The music you choose should allow you to show technical and expressive control as a performer as well as an understanding of the music. Remember that some types of music, such as technical studies, easy arrangements and certain styles of pop music, tend to focus on a limited range of techniques and so may not give you much chance to show what you can do as a performer. Music that offers some contrasts in mood and the opportunity to show different types of technical skill is likely to serve you best.

The same considerations apply if you choose to include your own composition(s) – the music needs to give you the scope to show a good range of performing skills, which may be difficult if it is technically quite simple.

Think carefully about the order of the programme. A good plan is to start with a short piece that you know really well to give you confidence. Follow this with something that is longer and/or more demanding – don't leave difficult works to the end, when you are likely to start feeling tired. Finish with a short, bright work – perhaps a favourite 'party piece' that has been successful in the past – to bring your programme to a sparkling conclusion.

Difficulty level

Edexcel expects the pieces performed for this unit to be of about Grade 6 standard, although they do not have to come from the lists of pieces specified for grade examinations. Your teacher will be able to advise you on the difficulty level of specific pieces. In addition, the A2 Music section of the Edexcel website includes a booklet listing the difficulty levels of many different pieces.

A little extra credit is available if you give a good performance of music that is of a higher standard than Grade 6. If you present an item that is of a lower standard than Grade 6, it will not be possible to get the maximum marks available for that piece.

Whatever your technical standard it is better to choose music that you can perform with confidence, rather than attempt a difficult work which stretches your technique to its limit. Difficult pieces that are marred by hesitations or even breakdowns are likely to score far fewer marks than more modest pieces played really musically. The exam reports issued each year by Edexcel have consistently warned that many candidates choose over-ambitious programmes. Try not to fall into this trap yourself, but remember that a *little* adrenalin arising from performing a piece which is a challenge, but not an insuperable obstacle, may bring out your best work, providing that you are well prepared.

Note that you can omit repeats in your performance and shorten long sections that consist purely of accompaniment, but it is not acceptable to cut passages because they happen to be too difficult or to stop in the middle of a movement because it is too long. In such cases it would be better to choose a different work.

Accompaniment

If the music is intended to have an accompaniment (as will be the case for most music apart from that for piano and other chordal instruments) then it must be played with the accompaniment.

Try to work with an accompanist who can rehearse with you regularly, or at least on several occasions before the day. Even the most skilful accompanist will need to rehearse with you in advance if the performance is to be a success.

Unless you are performing in an ensemble, the accompaniment should normally be played by just one person on a contrasting instrument. This will usually be a piano but other combinations are allowed – for example, a flute solo could be accompanied on an acoustic guitar or a jazz saxophone solo could be supported by a double bass. You can use a pre-recorded (or sequenced) backing if it is appropriate for the style of music, provided that your own part is performed live and can be clearly distinguished. This is often a good option for electric guitarists and rock drummers.

Ensemble performing

You can, if you wish, perform as a member of an ensemble for this unit. If you choose to do so, note that there must not be more than five performers in the group, including yourself, and your own part must be clearly audible and not doubled by anyone else. Suitable ensembles include wind trios, string or vocal quartets, and small rock groups. You can include both solo and ensemble items in your programme if you wish, but there are no additional marks available for doing so and it could prove more difficult to organise the necessary resources.

A useful book which gives many ideas for getting the best out of ensemble performing of all kinds is *Rehearse, Direct and Play* by William Lloyd and Paul Terry, published by Musonix (www.musonix.co.uk).

Scores

You will have to submit a photocopy (not the original copy) of the music you perform for this unit. Only your own part is required, not the accompaniment or the parts for others in the case of an ensemble.

If your performance is improvised, as often occurs in jazz and rock music, you will still need to submit something on paper that will allow your work to be followed. If a score in conventional stave notation is not available this could be a lead sheet, chord chart, track sheet, table or diagram, together with a description of what is being attempted in improvised passages.

Similarly, if you perform your own composition(s), make sure that the score is as detailed as possible, and accurately reflects your performance.

Preparation

Having chosen and studied your piece(s) with your teacher, and practised to a standard that you feel is acceptable, it is essential that you try out the music under performance conditions – not to your instrumental teacher, parents or anyone else who has heard you working on the music week by week, but to someone who is able to hear the performance fresh. This could be a visiting relative, your fellow students, or another teacher at your school or college.

A small slip or two in this trial performance should not concern you greatly, but if you find that you often hesitate in the more difficult passages, it is an indication that you may have chosen something which might be too difficult. This means that you will need to decide if the work is viable or whether it would be better to make a more realistic choice.

In planning the run-up to the performance allow much more time than you think you are likely to need. Illness may curtail practice time and other commitments may prevent adequate rehearsal with accompanists or other members of an ensemble.

Try to have a run-through of the music in the venue in which you will be performing. If it is a large hall you will probably find that you need to project the sound and exaggerate the contrasts much more than when practising at home. Conversely if you are playing a loud instrument (brass or electric guitar, for example) in a small room, you will almost certainly need to limit louder dynamics.

Decide where you are going to sit or stand and check that the lighting is adequate but not dazzling. If you have an accompanist make sure that you have good eye contact without having to turn away from your listeners. If the piano is an upright, it may take some experimentation to find the best position. If you play an instrument that needs tuning before you start, plan how you are going to do this and remember that tuning is not necessarily something that all accompanists are able to help with.

Whether the piece is accompanied or not, spend some time trying out the opening in various ways. For pieces with a tricky start it can be easier to set the right speed by thinking of a more straightforward phrase from later in the piece and establishing a mental image of the right tempo from that.

The performance

On the day make sure you leave time for a warm-up. Check that you have to hand any extra equipment you might need (mutes, guitar foot-stools, spare strings and so on). If you require a music stand, check that you know how it is adjusted and secured – collapsing music stands are good for comedy acts but they can seriously undermine your confidence in a performance.

At the performance, there must be an audience of at least one person, in addition to the performer(s) and the teacher assessing your work, but there can be more if you wish. If there is to be an audience of any size, practise walking on stage and setting up, and plan how you will react to applause. Listeners will be disappointed if you shamble on at the start and rush off at the end. Audiences need plenty of time to show their appreciation: a hurried nod in their direction as you leave will appear clumsy, if not downright rude. If there is no printed programme, announce each piece in a positive and friendly manner before you perform it.

Expect to be a little nervous but remember that the more experience you can get of performing to others during the course, the more natural and enjoyable it will become. Blind panic will only normally set in if the music is under-rehearsed or too difficult and this, as we have explained, can be avoided by selecting suitable music and preparing it thoroughly.

How is the performance marked?

Each piece (or movement) that you perform is awarded up to eight marks in each of the following categories:

1. Quality of outcome: security and effectiveness, interpretation and communication; reaction to other parts in an ensemble; sufficient minimum length

2. Accuracy of pitch and rhythm

3. Continuity: fluency and control of tempo

4. Tone and technique, including any specific matters that are appropriate, such as bowing, intonation, pedalling

5. Phrasing, articulation and dynamics.

In the case of improvisation, marks in category 2 are awarded for the use of the stimulus in the performance; marks in category 3 are awarded for the coherence of the work (structure and balance), and marks in category 5 are awarded for use of instrument or voice (including appropriate range of timbre and management of texture).

The mark out of 40 for each piece is balanced against an overall mark for its total impression, and the total is adjusted if the piece is above the standard Grade 6 difficulty level.

Each piece is marked in the same way, and then an average mark out of 40 for the entire group of pieces is calculated. Finally, a mark out of 10 is added to reflect the quality of the performance as a whole, including the suitability and order of the pieces in creating a coherent yet contrasting programme. The complete unit is therefore marked out of 50.

A good mark requires technically secure performing, although the occasional well-covered slip that can happen in even the best-regulated performances should not be a matter of great concern. However, if your performance lacks fluency and coordination, perhaps being marred by stumbles, poor intonation or inability to maintain the correct speed, it is unlikely to be awarded a satisfactory mark. You can avoid this danger by choosing simpler music in which you have mastered the technical challenges and can therefore concentrate on communicating a really musical performance with good tone, effective and appropriate contrasts, and a sense of the style of the music.

It will help if you have a clear image of what you are trying to put across in your performance. You might, for instance, wish to convey rhythmic energy, a dreamy atmosphere, elegant phrasing, dramatic contrasts or subtle blends. Focus on expressive detail throughout the music. Rather than thinking of a passage as merely 'happy', try to decide if you mean boisterous, contented, frivolous, celebratory, cheeky or just cheerful. If it is 'sad', do you mean tragic, doom-laden, nostalgic, angry or solemn? Then try to evoke the moods you intend in your interpretation of the piece, whether it be the glittering ballroom of a minuet, the moonlit night of a nocturne or the smoky languor of a blues club. Never be content with merely 'getting the notes right'.

Unit 5: Composition and Technical Study

Requirements

For this unit you have to submit two pieces of work, which can be either:

➢ Two compositions (from different areas of study), or

➢ Two technical studies, or

➢ One composition and one technical study.

Edexcel will set briefs for compositions and tasks for technical studies. You have to complete your submissions in time to send to an examiner in May of your examination year. The final writing-up of your work has to be completed under controlled conditions.

The composition briefs

Edexcel will set four composition briefs in September at the start of your A2 course. Each is linked to one of the two areas of study (Instrumental Music and Applied Music) that also form the focus of your work for Unit 6. Here are the main choices (we will look at detailed examples later):

➢ Instrumental Music **Topic 1: Development and contrast**
A composition in which you will need to devise and vary short motifs in order to develop a longer structure.

➢ Instrumental Music **Topic 2: Exploiting instruments**
A composition in which you will need to write technically challenging music for acoustic instruments.

➢ Applied Music **Topic 3: Music for film and television**
A composition to accompany the events in a given scene.

➢ Applied Music **Topic 4: Music, dance and theatre**
A composition intended primarily for the world of dance.

Your composition should be about three minutes long and, unless directed otherwise in the brief, you are allowed to write it in any style and for whatever resources you wish, including parts for voices. However, be aware that marks are awarded for your use of forces and textures: it may prove difficult to achieve credit for a range of textures if you write for very slender resources, such as an unaccompanied flute.

If you submit two compositions, each must be about three minutes in length and each **must** come from a *different* area of study – in other words, you must choose either Topic 1 or 2 for the first piece, and either Topic 3 or 4 for the second.

Once the work is finished you will have to submit a detailed score, either hand-written or computer-printed. Stave notation should be used if this is the convention for the style that you have chosen.

If you are intending to submit two technical studies, turn to page 28.

Note that if you submit two pieces, each must last about three minutes. You should not submit a six-minute package made up of one long work and one much shorter one.

However, other forms of notation are acceptable if they are sufficiently detailed and more usual for the type of music you have created. For example, a pop or jazz composition might be presented as a lead sheet (melody and chord symbols); an electronic piece might be shown as a detailed track diagram, or a work in an experimental style might be notated as a prose score (a detailed table of instructions) or in graphic form.

Whatever type of score you decide upon, it is important to show as much musical detail as possible. For instance, if you use guitar tab, indicate the rhythms you want and add a few words to show the style – the same applies if you use guitar grids (or frames, as they are sometimes called) for the chords.

> For more on guitar tab and guitar grids, see the *AS Music Literacy Workbook* by Rebecca Berkley, Rhinegold, 2009, ISBN 978-1-906178-46-8.

You will also have to submit a recording of the composition on audio CD or MiniDisc. This can either be of a live performance or it can be a studio-based recording. If the necessary resources are not available, you are allowed to submit a recording of an arrangement or a synthesised version. Whatever route you take, try to ensure that the recording matches the score as closely as possible. Although the quality of the recording is not assessed, it plays a valuable role in showing the examiner what you intend, especially if your score doesn't consist of detailed stave notation.

You do *not* have to submit a sleeve note for your A2 composition(s), as you did for the AS Composing unit.

It is important to spend time practising your general composing skills before starting on the brief, and to continue to do so while working on it. Your score for the brief itself has to be completed under controlled conditions, for which you are allowed 14 hours (not 15 hours, as at AS). You are allowed 28 hours in total for completing the scores if you choose to submit two compositions.

> You must complete the score of your composition under supervision during the 14 hours described as 'controlled conditions'. However, you are allowed to research and prepare ideas for the piece outside this time. Your teacher will explain how controlled conditions will be run in your school or college.

Additional time is allowed for recording the work, but if you then need to make any changes to the score, these must be completed under controlled conditions, within whatever is left of your 14 hours. It is therefore best not to leave the recording until all your supervised time has been used up.

Research and preparation for the brief, including listening to and studying relevant music, does not have to be done under controlled conditions, but your teacher is required to check that any rough drafts or sketches that you use when working on your final score are your own work.

Your submissions for this unit need to be completed in time to send to the examiner by the specified date, which is likely to be in the middle of May.

Getting started

Once you have chosen a brief, you can do some valuable research and planning before starting to use up your supervised time on the actual process of composing. Listen carefully and analytically to plenty of relevant music and start to gather information about the resources you intend to use.

It is important to study as many models as you can for the brief you choose, as this will provide you with a variety of ideas on how to go about structuring and developing your own piece. There may be suitable works to study in NAM, which you are allowed to consult while working on your own piece. Other ideas for related listening are included in the sample briefs later in this chapter, but obviously you will need to find pieces that are relevant to your own chosen brief.

When studying other music it is important to realise that you are not expected to write in the style of any specific composer. You should instead be looking at the ways in which composers:

➢ Begin and end a piece

➢ Establish and develop ideas

➢ Create specific moods

➢ Introduce contrasts (of key, mood, timbre or texture)

➢ Design material to suit the characteristics of the instruments and voices concerned

➢ Use structure – not just a form, such as theme and variations, but also how the music is paced to include areas of tension and relaxation, and points of climax

➢ Unify their music, so that it sounds like a satisfying whole rather than a succession of unrelated ideas.

Getting the right balance between unity and diversity is one of the most important tasks for a composer. Too much repetition and the piece will sound boring. Too many new ideas and it will not gel. Careful listening to a broad range of relevant music will show you how composers throughout the ages have evolved many different solutions to this problem.

Resources

You will need to decide on the resources you are going to use for your piece. If other performers are to be involved it is best to write for people who will be available to work with you during the whole composing process, so other students in your group would be the obvious choice.

Start by planning how the characteristics of the instruments and/ or voices might best be exploited. Try to identify the skills (and weaknesses) of each performer so that you can use their individual strengths in your composing. You could discuss what sorts of things are easy and what are difficult for each instrument or voice – although improvising, both separately and together, is often much quicker and more productive than using words.

Your research should also include the ranges and characteristics of the instruments and/or voices you intend to use. Reread pages 14–19 of the *Edexcel AS Music Study Guide* for a discussion of some of the matters to consider when writing for different types of instrument.

Understanding the composition brief

In this section we shall look at an example of each of the four types of brief, and discuss how it might be tackled.

Instrumental Music Topic 1

Development and contrast

The focus of this brief will be a composition in which you have to create a musical structure by developing and/or varying a musical idea. Here is an example of the type of brief that could be set:

Compose a piece in which two or more themes are developed and contrasted. You could use a conventional structure, such as rondo form, but you are free to adopt whatever structure you wish for the piece.

The key to successfully developing a musical idea is to begin with something very short but rhythmically distinctive. Perhaps the most famous example is the first movement of Beethoven's 5th Symphony, in which the opening four-note motif develops into some 500 bars of music. At the start it is announced *ff* in octaves, but there is an immediate contrast in dynamic and texture as Beethoven recasts the motif as a succession of quiet imitative entries:

Beethoven, Symphony No. 5 (i)

Straight after this passage Beethoven fills in the interval of a falling 3rd, but keeps the rhythm the same, and then alternates this new version of the opening motif with its own inversion (in which the intervals rise rather than fall), forming the dialogue between upper parts shown in (a) *below*.

The brevity of the motif allows it to be developed into figures that cascade down diminished 7th chords (b) and punctuate the music with perfect cadences at climactic moments (c):

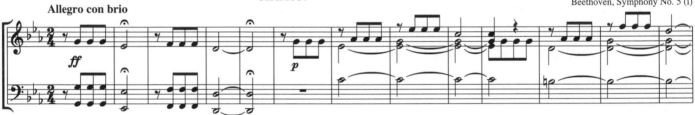

After 58 bars Beethoven introduces what at first might appear to be a contrasting theme:

However, it begins with a new version of the opening motif, which is then expanded by the addition of extra notes and is accompanied by the familiar rhythm of the opening motif at its cadence.

Short motifs are often repeated when they first appear. In the next example, by Mendelssohn, a one-bar motif using notes from the tonic chord is repeated to form a two-bar unit. This is then balanced by two bars that outline chord V⁷ to complete a four-bar phrase:

A repeated motif can be varied in:

➤ Dynamic (the repeat could be quieter, like an echo),

➤ Register (it could appear in a different octave, perhaps even in the bass), or

➤ Timbre (it could be assigned to a different instrument).

Repeating a motif is a good thing to do after its first appearance, but repetition is not development. Once an idea has been established, it needs to develop – in other words, to change in pitch or rhythm (or both). One of the simplest means of development is sequence. Here, a three-note motif is repeated and then extended to two bars. After the crotchet rest, this opening is repeated a step lower to form a two-bar sequence:

This is called a diatonic sequence because all of the notes have been kept within the same key. If *every* note had moved down by exactly one tone, the last two pitches would have been E♭–C.

A diatonic sequence is good for establishing the key at the start of a composition (notice how the one above suggests chords I and V⁷) but an exact sequence can be more useful later in a piece to give a sense that the music is developing and moving forward, since it opens up the possibility of modulating to a different key:

Another way of developing a motif into a tune is to increase the size of one or more of its intervals (a process known as melodic augmentation). Often, as here, one pitch serves as an 'anchor' to which the tune frequently returns:

It is often possible to make a number of changes to a motif without losing its identity, providing it has a strong basic shape. The next

Remember that you are not expected to write music in the style of composers such as Beethoven nor to write a piece as long as a symphony! The examples in this section are intended to show you how studying techniques used in the past can help you find ways in which to develop your own ideas into longer melodies and sections.

An exact sequence like this is known as a 'real sequence'. This particular example is a 'modulating sequence' that begins in A major and then moves a tone higher to B minor.

example shows just a few of the ways in which the opening motif from Mendelssohn's *Hebrides* Overture is developed later in the movement:

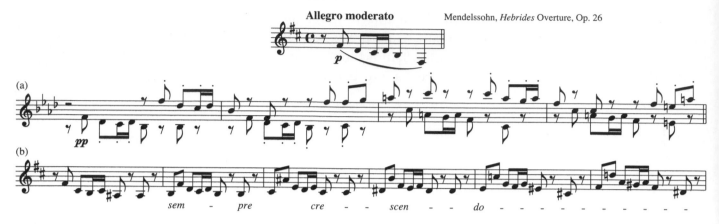

This works well because the ear notices the rhythm of a motif at least as clearly as its pitches, which is why it is worth spending time devising rhythmically strong main ideas in your own work.

In the next example, the pitches of (b) are only loosely related to those in (a), and yet the distinctive rhythm ensures that we hear it as a development of the opening tune:

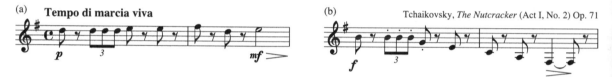

There are many other ways to develop an idea, but we will end by looking at just two other common methods.

The first is more like variation rather than true development, because it simply involves decorating a melody. Nevertheless, if you compare the two bracketed phrases *below*, you can see that some of the notes from the first phrase have been subtly nudged into different places in the bar in the second phrase to achieve a very elegant sense of development:

The second is a process known as fragmentation, in which a part of a melodic idea is detached and then developed in its own right. Here, a two-bar motif is repeated in sequence (bars 3–4) and then bar 4 is developed in a sequence of its own (bar 5–6):

Later in the movement, Beethoven fragments this material still further, isolating just the turn-like triplet figure:

You may have noticed that almost all of the advice on this topic has focused on development rather than contrast. This is because unifying a composition, so that all of its sections sound as though they belong to the same piece, is the more difficult task. Writing contrasting passages is relatively easy, but they need to have a logical relationship with what has gone before, and not sound as if a totally different piece has interrupted your work. Remember that contrast achieved through changes of key, instrumentation and texture can be more effective than introducing *totally* new musical material. Think about making connections and carefully plan the transition from one section to the next.

Studying pieces such as those from which the examples in this section have been taken should form an important part of your research. You will pick up many tips on how to develop ideas and how to link contrasting sections, in whatever style you choose to write. Be aware that if you write in a style such as minimalism, in which repetition plays an important role, it is essential that your musical ideas constantly grow and mutate – simple repetition will not be enough for a topic based on development and contrast.

Exploiting instruments

The title of this topic means making the best possible use of the instrument(s) for which you write by bringing out their most effective musical qualities. It is an extension of Composing Topic 2 ('Composing idiomatically for instruments') in AS Music, so you should find the advice given on pages 14–19 and 20–21 of the *Edexcel AS Music Study Guide* useful as a starting point.

Like the AS task, electronic pieces are not suitable for this topic, although you are allowed to submit a synthesised recording if suitable live players are not available. However, if you do this, take great care to check that your work is playable on the acoustic instrument(s) concerned.

The composition brief will indicate what is required, which could involve writing technically challenging material, using particular instrumental techniques or demonstrating other qualities of the instrument, such as its ability to maintain a lyrical line. Here is an example of the type of brief that could be set:

Compose a fantasy for one melody instrument accompanied by piano, or for two or three melody instruments. It should exploit the potential of the chosen forces and include contrasting sections (for example, a lyrical opening leading to a solo cadenza, and rounded off with a brilliant finale).

A fantasy (or *fantasia* in Italian) is, in the sense used here, a piece which simply follows the composer's imagination or fancy, and doesn't have a set form. A cadenza is an extended solo, usually unaccompanied, sometimes improvised, and often placed towards the end of a movement.

Composers have used a wide variety of titles for display pieces, including pictorial descriptions (such as 'The Flight of the Bumble Bee'). Some common terms for various types include:

Instrumental Music Topic 2

Toccata (from the Italian *toccare*, meaning 'to touch') – a fast piece designed to show off rapid finger movement

Study (or, in French, *étude*) – a piece designed to show off one or more particular aspects of technique, such as staccato tonguing on a wind instrument or double-stopping on a string instrument

Impromptu ('unprompted') – a piece without a set form, often intended to sound as though it is improvised

Capriccio – another type of piece without a set form, in which the composer seems to follow his own caprice or whim

Perpetuum mobile ('perpetual motion') – a piece based on a fast and continuous stream of notes, sometimes with repeats arranged so that it seems never to reach a definite stopping place.

Of course, if an unusual term appears in the brief, you will have plenty of time to research its meaning before starting work on your composition.

Your research should also include detailed study of works in which instrumental technique plays an important role, such as:

> For reasons of space, we can only give a few suggestions for study here. When conducting your own research, try entering into a web search engine 'virtuoso music for' followed by the name of the instrument concerned – this is likely to produce a wide range of resources, including technically challenging music in styles as diverse as gypsy music and Indian music, as well as pieces from the jazz, rock and classical repertoire.

Bach's Toccata and Fugue in D minor for organ
The Toccata from Widor's Organ Symphony No. 5
Chopin's 'Raindrop' Prelude, Op. 28 No. 15 for piano
Chopin's 'Revolutionary' *Étude*, Op. 10 No. 12 for piano
Alkan's *Le festin d'Ésope*, Op. 39 No. 12 for piano
Paganini's Caprice in A minor, Op. 1 No. 24 for solo violin
Ian Clarke's *Zoom Tube* for solo flute
Berio's *Sequenza IX* for solo clarinet
Arban's Variations on 'The Carnival of Venice' for solo cornet
Tárrega's *Recuerdos de la Alhambra* for acoustic guitar
Joe Satriani's album 'One Big Rush' for electric guitar
Rimsky-Korsakov's 'The Flight of the Bumble Bee'
    (arranged for various instruments).

When planning your own composition, think carefully about the techniques that you could explore. These include using the full range of the instrument, perhaps contrasting the tone colours that are available in different registers. Various types of articulation could be explored, as well as different types of melodic patterns, and the use of specific techniques, such as pizzicato, mutes, piano pedalling, electronic effects for the guitar and so on.

If the brief doesn't suggest a structure, variation form can be useful for this topic. Whatever you decide, remember that the composition needs to work well as a piece of music, with a sense of development and points of climax and repose – it should be more than just a showcase for a succession of different techniques.

Applied Music Topic 3   ## Music for film and television

The brief for this topic will focus on writing music for the moving image. It could specify a piece (known as an underscore) suitable to accompany a given scenario, or it might ask for a title theme and perhaps a succession of short extracts to be used in a documentary or other type of television programme.

The brief will consist of a simple written description – you won't be provided with visual images on DVD. Similarly, you are not required to synchronise your music to any type of visual image or to submit video clips with your work. However, where the brief involves writing music for a given scenario, you are encouraged to add comments to your score to show where the music is designed to illustrate specific visual images. Here is an example of the type of brief that could be set:

Compose music to underscore a short film about the effects of global warming on an idyllic Pacific island. It starts with pictures of holiday-makers on sun-drenched beaches, then cuts to a simulation of the disasters that occur when sea levels rise. It ends with pictures of the islanders leaving their tropical paradise forever.

In this topic, the structure of the music is likely to be dictated by the scenario in the brief, so you will not necessarily need to think in terms of conventional musical forms. Our example suggests a three-part structure that might begin with warm, exotic colours, leading to passages of great turbulence, and rounded off by a sad and nostalgic section.

Although a brief like this is likely to result in a work of changing moods to reflect the visual images, it is important not to let your composition become a series of unconnected episodes or sound effects. Think how you might be able to use a small number of motifs that can change as the drama unfolds but that also serve to unify the work as a whole. Some of the suggestions on developing motifs on pages 16–18 should help in giving you ideas.

Research for this topic could include study of the six extracts of film and television music in NAM (although be aware that some of these are arrangements rather than original underscores) and the use of music in extended television advertisements. Other famous pieces of film music to explore might include:

Psycho (1960). Bernard Hermann's score for this classic horror film uses only strings, paralleling director Alfred Hitchcock's decision to restrict his palette to black and white film. The 'shower scene' is famous for the way in which terror is portrayed by screechingly dissonant violins rather than by precise images of the murder.

> For more on film music, including discussion of a number of famous soundtracks, see *Film Music in Focus* by David Ventura, Rhinegold, 2010, ISBN 978-1-907447-08-2.

The Magnificent Seven (1960), with a score by Elmer Bernstein (unrelated to Leonard Bernstein) that is highly typical of the music that has become associated with the epic American western.

The Good, the Bad and the Ugly (1966). Another classic western, but Ennio Morricone's style is very different from Elmer Bernstein's, having a modal main theme, unusual instruments such as the ocarina and harmonica, wordless voices and whistling.

Jaws (1975). John Williams' score for this thriller is famous for a simple two-note ostinato that represents the killer shark. Williams uses this motif persistently to signal approaching danger and he avoids using it when there is a false alarm of a shark attack. But having thus conditioned his audience, later scenes in which the huge jaws surge up from the water become even more frightening because they occur without any musical warning.

Chariots of Fire (1981) with music by Vangelis is an early example of a soundtrack written for entirely synthetic sounds.

Batman (1989) has a dark and dramatic score by Danny Elfman that also reveals the composer's love of musical irony. Batman himself is associated with a five-note motif in a minor key, while major-key music accompanies the evil Joker, whose death is preceded by a macabre roof-top waltz.

The Da Vinci Code (2006). Hans Zimmer's sombre score draws on a wide variety of resources, ranging from the combination of electric violin and acoustic cello in the title sequence to massive choral effects that underpin the religious overtones in this controversial murder mystery.

When you study film music, observe how composers react to a variety of stock dramatic situations such as love scenes, tragedy, comedy, horror, chases and fights. Also take note of how music can be used to 'paint' pictures of different types of landscape and seascape in various moods – tranquil, stormy, bathed in sunlight or threatened by storms – and how they sometimes draw on features of older music to suggest an historical period. Pay special attention to the ways in which composers move from one mood to another, since this is something you will almost certainly have to do in your own composition.

Applied Music Topic 4 — Music, dance and theatre

This brief is potentially very wide-ranging, since it could involve writing music for:

➢ Social dancing (from classic ballroom dancing, through salsa and other Latin-American dances to modern night-club styles involving the use of music technology)

➢ Performance in a theatre – which could mean formal ballet, contemporary dance, or a dance sequence for a musical or an opera (possibly including voices, if you wish)

➢ Performance in a concert or for playing for pleasure at home, based on dance styles but not intended for actual dancing.

The brief is likely to give you reasonable flexibility, although it is worth noting that Edexcel's sample brief for this topic requires the composition to show the influence of a non-Western style. This could be Asian-inspired Bhangra or a Latin-American style such as the tango, but there is nothing to stop you exploring some more unusual enthusiasm, such as African ritual dance, dance for the classical Chinese theatre or the Hawaiian sacred dance known as hula. Providing it is well executed, examiners are always likely to enjoy the work of candidates who explore beyond the obvious!

Whatever is set by Edexcel, you will have plenty of time between receiving the brief and starting on your own work to research any unusual requirements. Here is an example of the sort of brief that could be set:

Compose a piece of dance music based on the idea of conflict and resolution. It could be designed as a number to appear in a musical or modern opera, or it could be intended for professional dancers to present in a dance studio or at an arts festival.

A brief like this can be realised in a number of ways. No particular style is mentioned, so you could write a piece of electronic music for the dancers to use as a backing track. This would be fine for use in a dance studio, but in the theatre live musicians are normally employed. If the work is intended to form part of a contemporary opera, you might choose to write in a dissonant Modernist style, or perhaps in a gentler Postmodernist or Minimalist style. However, if the dance is to form part of a musical, a lighter, possibly rock-based, style would be more appropriate.

Much dance music, especially for social dancing, has a clearly defined beat, with phrases of equal lengths, and often quite a lot of repetition. Structures are generally simple – for example, verse and chorus form or various types of rondo, such as ABACABA – and variety is often achieved by thinning out the texture in some sections rather than by introducing highly contrasting material. However, professional dancers are used to much more complex rhythm patterns, allowing composers to be more adventurous.

As with the other topics, preparation should include the study of relevant examples. For dance music, these could include:

Stravinsky's three early ballet scores (*The Firebird*, *Petrushka* and *The Rite of Spring*), along with his Neoclassical score for *Pulcinella* (excerpts of the concert suite from the ballet are in NAM 7).

Prokofiev's ballet *Romeo and Juliet*, one number from which ('The Dance of the Knights') has become well known through its use as the title music for the television series 'The Apprentice'.

The Three-Cornered Hat by Manuel de Falla, much of it inspired by flamenco and the many other types of Spanish folk music that influenced the work.

Witty French ballet music, such as Satie's *Parade*, Milhaud's *Le Boeuf sur le Toit* and Poulenc's *Les Biches* (all revealing a rich mix of influences from music hall and circus music to Latin-American styles, ragtime and early jazz).

Copland's *Rodeo*, which incorporates cowboy tunes, dances in unusual rhythms and the popular 'Hoe Down' in barn-dance style.

Britten's *The Prince of the Pagodas*, which is influenced by Balinese gamelan music.

'Still Life' at the Penguin Café – a ballet with an ecological message about endangered species and a witty score by Simon Jeffes that reflects Latin rhythms, elements of folk and pop music, and aspects of Minimalism.

Dance has played an important role in many musicals. In some cases dance numbers are included as an excuse to add to the colour and spectacle of the show, but dance is more effective when it forms an integral part of the plot. An early example is Richard Rodgers' *On Your Toes* (1936), in which the story about classical ballet meeting the world of jazz enabled dance to be introduced in a way that enhances, rather than interrupts, the drama.

Most of Rodgers' later musicals include dance numbers, notably *Oklahoma!* (1943), in which dance is used to further the action and develop the audience's understanding of the characters and their motivation. In addition to songs that develop into dance routines and a big set-piece Barn Dance in Act 2, the first act ends with a 15-minute 'dream sequence' in which premonitions of the future are acted out in modern ballet.

Production numbers centred on dance can be found in many musicals over the following decades, including Frederick Loewe's *My Fair Lady* (1956), Jerry Bock's *Fiddler on the Roof* (1964) and John Kander's *Cabaret* (1966). Dance is used to convey the action in almost every important scene of Marvin Hamlisch's *A Chorus Line* (1975), while act two of Lloyd Webber's *Song and Dance* (1982) is based on dance, just as the first act is based on song.

In the last quarter of the 20th century dance tended to give way to impressive technical effects in many of the 'mega musicals' of the age, but it is central to works such as Elton John's *Billy Elliott: the Musical* (2005).

In the 21st century, musicals based on back catalogues of pop songs have become popular, the most famous being *Mamma Mia!* (2001), which uses the hits of ABBA. These works, known as 'compilation musicals' or 'jukebox musicals', tend to have a slender plot, but are filled out with bright dance sequences in the style of pop videos.

The musical most closely associated with dance is undoubtedly Leonard Bernstein's *West Side Story* (1957). Bernstein had already written for contemporary dancers in his ballet *Fancy Free* and its spin-off, the musical *On the Town* (both 1944). He worked with the same choreographer (Jerome Robbins) on *West Side Story*, in which much of the drama is conveyed in dance. Instead of an overture, the work opens with a prologue in which the tension between rival gangs is conveyed in mime choreographed to music. The 'Dance at the Gym' forms a showcase of challenge dances between the rivals, and the casting of one of the gangs as Puerto-Rican immigrants gave Bernstein the opportunity to base various song-and-dance numbers on the rhythms of popular Latin-American dances.

If the brief allows you to write music intended for social dancing, there could be a number of options. The main types of ballroom dance in use today include the waltz, foxtrot and quickstep as well as Latin-American styles such as the tango, samba, rumba, paso doble and cha cha. In Latin nightclubs, salsa is the most popular style, along with dances such as the lambada and the merengue. In other nightclubs, dance music could range from disco and hip-hop to styles such as house, techno and trance.

Other types of social dance include styles that have developed from folk music and which often involve group dances rather than partner dances. In country and western, for example, the line dance and the square dance are the two standard forms. Many communities maintain their own local dance traditions, such as the reels, jigs and strathspeys of Scottish country dancing, or Bhangra, which began as Punjabi folk music but which is now often heard in a more westernised form in Britain.

In general, all such dances have a characteristic speed, metre and rhythm pattern which needs to form a prominent feature of your own composition, and some have their own characteristic instrumentation.

Research to identify the main features of any dance style you are interested in can usefully begin on the internet, where recorded examples are also often available for study.

Working the composition brief

Writing the final score must be done under controlled conditions and within the 14 hours allowed, although you can (and should) practise general composing skills, research your chosen brief, study relevant music and make preliminary drafts outside this time. Remember that developing ideas and varying the texture will help you to achieve that really good mark you hope for.

Developing ideas

However good your main idea is, it needs to be developed so that the listener feels that the music is taking them on a journey. Too much repetition can easily become boring, but a constant stream of new material will sound confusing. Take time to explore your ideas in depth rather than introducing too much new material.

As well as striking the right balance between unity and diversity, plan clear areas of tension, relaxation and climax in your work. Study the methods used in music that you enjoy, and then apply the principles you discover to your own style of composing.

> Some minimalist and riff-based music is highly repetitive. If you choose one of these styles, think carefully about how you can achieve variety and a sense of development in your work. Be prepared to write a piece longer than the basic three minutes if you feel that greater length is needed in order to include these important features.

Varying the texture

A good variety of texture will enhance almost any style of music. If the tune is always allocated to the same instrument, accompanied by sustained chords in the other parts, the piece is likely to be dull to listen to and boring to play. Give all your resources a share in thematic material, and remember that presenting a tune in different octaves, or giving it to two instruments in unison or in octaves, will help create variety. Make accompaniments more interesting by basing them on distinctive rhythmic patterns and including the occasional melodic motif to complement the main tune.

If your piece is for four instruments, try giving one of them a rest in some sections, or alternate one pair of instruments with a different pair, and include a few totally unaccompanied phrases. Don't forget that each instrument can be used in different parts of its range for variety and that the use of well-contrasted dynamics and articulation will also make your work more interesting.

If you are writing a piece for solo instrument and piano, remember that the pianist can carry the tune in some sections, and doesn't have to be limited to accompaniment. Even if the piece is for piano alone, remember that the tune could sometimes be in the bass, or it could be presented in bare octaves (without chords), and that passages for both hands in the treble clef (or both in the bass clef) can offer a very effective contrast.

Other ways to maintain variety include splitting a long melody between different instruments and adding a countermelody or other point of contrapuntal interest. If phrase-endings on a long note cause the pace to flag, consider adding a link (or 'fill') to propel the music forward, or, alternatively, see if the start of the new phrase could overlap with the end of the previous one.

Plan the pacing of your work carefully. For example, a climax can be supported by thickening the texture, increasing the rate of change of the harmony (and perhaps adding a dominant pedal) and introducing greater rhythmic activity, as well as by more obvious means such as ascending to a high note and getting louder.

Above all, though, remember that rests are the key to achieving good variety of texture. If all of your players are occupied in every bar and there are few rests, there is unlikely to be enough variety of texture in your composition.

How is composition marked?

The mark scheme is basically the same as that used for composing at AS, although expectations will be higher at A2 than at AS in each of the mark categories listed below. If you submit two compositions, each will be marked in a similar way.

The examiner will give a mark for overall impression created by the piece, and will balance this against marks for five of the six categories below – the first three, plus whichever two of the last three are most appropriate for the composition concerned:

1. Quality of ideas and outcome. To do well, your composition needs to sound convincing and complete, with some exciting musical ideas. If it is less than three minutes in length, you risk receiving a low mark in this category.

2. Coherence. To do well, your composition needs to have a well thought-out structure, with a balance of unity and diversity, so that the work is neither over-repetitive nor so full of unrelated ideas that it fails to hang together.

3. Forces and textures. To do well, you need to write effectively and sympathetically for the resources you have chosen and you need to include a good variety of texture.

4. Harmony. To do well, your work should show a good grasp of harmonic progressions and treatment of dissonance (including a wider range of chords and perhaps more sophisticated use of modulation than was expected in the AS composing unit).

5. Melody. To do well, your melodies should be distinctive and have a good shape, with real sense of direction, and your part-writing should flow well.

6. Rhythm. To do well, your rhythms need to be imaginative and well controlled in all parts of the texture. Aim for a good balance between repetition to help unify the piece and variety to help differentiate contrasting sections.

As in the AS composing unit, you will be awarded marks for two categories out of harmony, melody and rhythm. This suggests that the full mark range would not be available for music with neither melody nor harmony, such as a piece for drum kit. If you are planning such a work, try to include melody and/or harmony parts, either for tuned percussion or for another instrument.

Using a computer

Some people find that developing compositions at a MIDI work-station can be a good way of working, even if the piece is destined for eventual performance by live musicians. Sequencer systems can also be useful to produce an approximation of a performance for recording purposes if live instrumentalists are unavailable.

However, the advice we gave in the *Edexcel AS Music Study Guide* also applies to composing at A2. MIDI software can give you little or no warning that what you write could be unplayable by live musicians – string chords which sound good on a synthesiser may be impossible on a violin, wind parts without breathing points that are no problem for a computer are unlikely to be possible for humans, and untransposed trumpet parts that descend into the bass clef will leave your trumpeter bewildered.

If you are using a sequencer to develop a piece for live players it will therefore be wise to try out ideas with the performers at an early stage.

Another potential drawback of computer-based composing is the ease with which 'copy and paste' can add extra sections to a piece. In music, repeated sections are frequently varied in some way – perhaps by being in a different key, or by having a different ending, or by being decorated in various ways, or by having changes made to the instrumentation and texture. Too many unaltered repeats runs the risk of a low mark for 'coherence'.

The score

Your score may be fully notated or, if appropriate to the style of the music, it could take the form of a lead sheet, chord chart, track diagram or annotated graphic. Whatever format you use, it should be clear and detailed, with numbered pages clipped together in the right order. Bar numbers, either at the start of each system or every ten bars, are a helpful addition to any score.

If the piece includes a number of different instruments, make sure the staves are labelled with instrument names at the start of every system, although abbreviations can be used after the opening. If you write the score by hand, it will help the layout if you leave a blank stave or two between systems. Remember that you can use conventional repeat signs in the score to avoid copying out identical sections of music.

Whatever type of score you submit, you should include full and clear directions to show how you want the music performed. However, there is nothing to be gained by using lots of Italian terms (English is perfectly acceptable) or by peppering the music with a

Remember that an entirely electronic piece is not suitable for Topic 2 (Exploiting instruments).

random selection of dynamics and phrase marks. All markings should relate clearly to the music.

Computer-generated scores

Using a computer to produce a score can give neat results if you have a good understanding of music notation and the software concerned. However, music notation programs can produce very inaccurate scores if left to their own devices. You need to be able to evaluate the results of what you see and adjust the settings if note lengths, rests, ties, beams or accidentals don't follow the normal conventions. Similarly, the use of incorrect clefs is likely to lead to the appearance of too many leger lines. Take particular care that the software correctly handles parts for instruments that are written an octave higher than they sound (such as the guitar, bass guitar and double bass).

Remember to add phrasing, articulation and dynamics, and check that staves are labelled with instrument names (not track numbers) or are identified as parts for sequenced sounds if you are writing an electronic studio piece.

You also need to know how your software handles repeats. It may well print the music out again in full, when what is really required is a repeat sign or a *da capo* direction, perhaps with first- and second-time bars for different endings.

Finally, check that the layout of the score is clear throughout. The stave size should allow for a reasonable number of bars per page, and there should be more than one system per page unless you are writing for a very large ensemble. Staves that contain only rests for an entire system can be omitted to save space – just printing two or three bars per page is a waste of paper and the examiner will find your work hard to follow if pages of the score have to be turned every few seconds. However, make sure that staves and systems are not so close together that leger lines or other symbols overlap.

The recording

Whichever brief you choose, the recording can be mocked up using sequenced and synthesised sounds if the musicians required are not available. Although the quality of the recording is not assessed, it plays a valuable role in showing the examiner what you intend, especially if your score is not in full stave notation.

The recording is made outside the 14 supervised hours allowed for completing the score. Remember that if you make changes at this stage, you won't get extra time for revising the score, so don't leave recording until after all your supervised time has been used up.

The technical study tasks

The technical studies are very different from the composing briefs, although there are a number of overlaps between the two skills. Each technical study involves completing a passage in a specified style, and so a thorough knowledge of harmony and the style concerned is required, as well as a good sense of melodic line and skill in part-writing. The three briefs are:

➤ **Topic 1: Baroque counterpoint**
The brief will consist of an exercise in two-part counterpoint for instruments from the Baroque period, in which you have to complete a bass part (with figuring) to harmonise the given melody in some bars, and to write a melody to fit the given figured bass in others.

➤ **Topic 2: Chorale**
The brief will consist of a chorale in four-part harmony, with some passages printed in full but with only the melody given elsewhere. You have to complete the harmonisation by adding parts for alto, tenor and bass voices.

➤ **Topic 3: Popular song**
The brief will consist of an exercise in ballad style, in which you will have to add a melody (without words) to fit the given bass part and chord symbols in some sections, and to supply a bass part and chord symbols to harmonise the given melody in others.

> Remember that you can choose two technical studies (and no composition) or two compositions (and no technical study), or one composition and one technical study.

Completing your coursework has to be done under controlled conditions. You are allowed a maximum of three hours for each technical study, during which time you are allowed to try out your work on a keyboard or computer equipped with headphones. The finished task is submitted as a score – no recording is required.

The specification states that technical studies will be issued in September (although you should check with your teacher that this remains the case). However, it is likely that you will only start work on the actual task(s) quite late in your course, as much time will first be needed to master the techniques involved and to work a number of preparatory exercises. These techniques would take an entire book of their own to explain, but fortunately a very good one is available: the *A2 Music Harmony Workbook* by Hugh Benham (Rhinegold, 2008, ISBN 978-1-906178-39-0) contains full information about each of the three briefs, along with tips, working methods and many preparatory and practice exercises.

> The *AS Music Harmony Workbook* by the same author will also be useful if you feel unsure about the basics of keys, chords and part-writing.

How are technical studies marked?

The examiner will give a mark for an overall impression of the work, and will balance this against marks for the following five elements:

1. Chords and keys. To do well, you need convincing harmonic progressions and a good understanding of modulation and the appropriate treatment of dissonance.

2. Realisation of, and adding, a figured bass (topic 1) or chord symbols (topic 3). To do well, this must be done accurately.

3. Sense of line. To do well, your melodic writing needs to have a good shape and a sense of purpose.

4. Part-writing. To do well, the individual lines in your work need to flow convincingly and without technical errors.

5. Style. To do well, you need to capture the characteristics of the specified style securely and creatively.

> In the case of Topic 2, marks in category 1 are awarded for chords and keys in the first half of the study and marks in category 2 are awarded for chords and keys in the second half.

Unit 6: Further Musical Understanding

Part A will take about 30 minutes, including the preliminary five minutes for reading the paper. It is suggested that you keep to less than 40 minutes for Part B and less than 50 minutes for Part C, in order to leave a little time for checking your answers at the end.

Requirements

This final unit is about listening to music and showing that you understand how it works. At the end of the course you will sit a two-hour exam paper, marked out of 90 and consisting of the three parts described *below*.

Part A is based on music that will almost certainly be unfamiliar, but that will be related in some way to works in NAM that you have studied. The music for this part will be played to you on CD. Parts B and C are based directly on the works from NAM that you will have studied. You will be able to refer to an unmarked copy of NAM during the exam.

Part A: Aural awareness (28 marks)

At the start of the exam you will have five minutes to read through the entire paper, after which the music for Part A will be played to you on CD. There are two main questions in this section.

Question 1 will involve comparing two excerpts of music. They will be played three times each (in the order A–B, A–B, A–B) and there will be no score to follow.

You will have to answer a series of short questions that will focus mainly on similarities and differences between the two extracts. These are likely to refer to resources (instruments and/or voices) and ask for comparisons in the way they are used. For example, you could be required to spot that one extract features a triadic melody for bassoon beneath a tremolo in the upper strings, while the other features a stepwise melody for saxophone supported by sustained chords from the brass.

In addition, you will be asked to place the music into its context, usually by suggesting the type of work from which it is taken, the name of a likely composer and the probable date when it was written (for more about this, see *below*).

Question 2 will consist of a single extract heard five times (with pauses between playings), for which there will be a skeleton score. You will have to:

➢ Notate a short section of the music you hear, such as a couple of bars of melody or bass

➢ Identify some chords (which could include chromatic chords such as the diminished 7th, augmented 6th and Neapolitan 6th)

➢ Recognise certain standard chord progressions (such as cadence patterns and the circle of 5ths)

➢ Identify one or more modulations to related keys (the relative minor or major, the dominant and its relative minor or major, and the subdominant and its relative minor or major).

Again, you are likely to be asked to suggest the type of work from which the extract is taken, and to name a likely composer and date when it was written.

Identifying specific features of the music is a skill that will be familiar from AS Music Unit 3, although now you will be working with unfamiliar extracts rather than with set works that you have studied. As with the part of question 2 that requires you to notate a short passage, you will need plenty of practice throughout the course on tests of this sort.

Practice listening papers are available from the publishers of this book, but you can also do much to help yourself by listening to music analytically whenever you get the chance. When you hear something unfamiliar, try to identify the type of ensemble and the instruments you hear – can you recognise any special effects such as muted brass or pitch bends on a guitar? Is the music in a major or minor key, or is it modal or atonal? What is the metre and is there anything particularly noticeable about the rhythm, such as dotted patterns, triplets or syncopation? How would you describe the shape of the melody? Is it diatonic or chromatic, and does it include any particular features such as wide leaps or appoggiaturas? What sorts of texture can be heard?

Detailed listening needs real concentration – it is not something that can be done while reading a magazine or texting – but the more you practise, the easier it will become. At the same time, try to widen your knowledge of repertoire. A good way to do this is to dip into Radio 3 or Classic FM's morning and teatime broadcasts and try to identify the music being played – check your answer when the presenter identifies the piece after it has finished.

At first, identifying style may seem difficult, but try to link features of the music you hear with other pieces that you know or are studying. There are various 'markers' that can help identify musical styles and periods. For example, if you hear a harpsichord and the melodies seem to be formed by spinning out short motifs to create long musical paragraphs, there is a good chance that the piece will be Baroque. Equally, if the rhythms seem irregular and the harmonies very dissonant, it is likely to be 20th-century.

Never rely on a single point of identification – you need to operate as a musical detective and sift all of the evidence to see which features support your conclusion and which perhaps contradict it.

As you build up a knowledge of different types of repertoire, identification will become easier, but be aware that at A2 you will usually be expected to identify quite narrow periods, such as early Baroque, mid-Baroque or late Baroque. However, remember that the music in Section A will be related in some way to the set works you have studied. If you know these thoroughly, it should help you make connections. For example, if your set works include NAM 16 (the quartet movement by Haydn), then one of the extracts could be from a symphony by Haydn or from a string quartet by a later composer. Remember that you will have an unmarked copy of NAM in the exam, in which you could quickly check any stylistic features of the recorded extracts that seem familiar.

Edexcel A2 Music Listening Tests by Hugh Benham and Alistair Wightman (ISBN 978-1-78038-064-3), and an accompanying CD, are available from www.musicroom.com.

You can listen to Classic FM live on the radio (100–102 FM), or on the internet at www.classicfm.co.uk.

You can listen to BBC Radio 3 live on the radio (90.3–92.3 FM) or on the internet at www.bbc.co.uk/radio3.

Both websites allow you to listen to programmes for some days after they were broadcast and to identify the music played.

Part A has to be answered first because that is when the CD will be played. The remaining questions can be tackled in whatever order you prefer, but keep an eye on the clock or you may run out of time – a sure way of missing valuable marks.

Part B: Music in context (26 marks)

This section will contain three questions on the group of set works from the 'Applied music' area of study that you have worked on during the course. You have to answer two of these, either in short notes or in continuous prose, spending about 20 minutes on each. Questions are likely to ask you to identify technical features of the music that contribute to its style, purpose or emotional impact. Sample questions are included at the end of the discussion on each of the set works later in this book, and some important points about writing answers are given *below*.

Part C: Continuity and change in instrumental music (36 marks)

In this section there will be two questions about the set works from the 'Instrumental music' area of study that you have worked on during the course. These will not be the same instrumental pieces that you studied for AS. You have to answer one of these questions by writing an essay, which will need to be completed in a little under 50 minutes.

Each of the questions will ask you to compare and contrast one or more musical features of *three* works. This could involve writing about form, texture, tonality, harmony, melody, metre and rhythm, or the resources used, showing what has remained similar over time, and what has differed. Sample questions are included at the end of the discussion on each group of instrumental works later in this book.

Analytical writing about music

At this level, examiners will hope to see that you can present clear and reasoned arguments in a logical way, supported by factual evidence and the accurate use of technical terminology. Although this may seem daunting at first, most of these skills are similar to those in any A-level subject where technical writing is involved and will be useful in later life whenever you have to write a report, an analysis, a proposal or any other similar document.

There are two important conventions in analytical writing that you should try to follow. Firstly, slang and colloquial expressions are never used, so we would always write 'Brahms varies the rhythm' rather than 'Brahms mucks around with the rhythm'.

Secondly, value judgements on how you perceive the worth of the music or its composer are normally avoided, so we wouldn't write something like 'Debussy's orchestration is better than Wagner's' or 'Mozart, the greatest Classical composer, created this masterful sonata …'. In fact, personal opinion in technical writing is seldom useful unless a question actually asks you for it – and even then, you should back up opinion with evidence. So, avoid expressions like 'Indian raga doesn't make sense to me'. A useful rule of thumb is to avoid personal pronouns (as in expressions such as 'I think', 'in my opinion' or 'you will see') and instead to write in a detached and objective style, since your subject should be the music itself rather than your reaction to it.

For much useful advice on technical writing about music for A level and beyond, see the *Writing About Music Workbook* by Alistair Wightman, Rhinegold, 2008, ISBN 978-1-906178-38-3.

So, what *will* help you gain an outstanding mark? In each of the Part B questions you need to make nine clear and relevant points (plus 18 in the essay for Part C), supported by references to precise locations in the score wherever possible. These references should take the form of bar numbers, along with beat numbers and the name of the part(s) concerned, if necessary. Don't waste time writing out the music, as examiners have their own copies of NAM.

Supplying evidence to support your points is one of the best ways to accumulate marks. You can save a lot of time if you know the score of each work thoroughly so that you can find examples to illustrate your arguments quickly.

Here are some other points to bear in mind:

1. Check that you really understand the question. It is likely to include technical terms such as tonality and texture that are often confused in the panic of an exam. Revise the information about the elements of music on pages 44–48 of the *Edexcel AS Music Study Guide* if you are at all unsure about such terms.

2. Only include points that are relevant to the question. If it asks about the style and texture of the music, you will get no marks for listing the instrumentation or writing about the composer and his other works, even if what you say is true.

3. Group your points logically. If the question asks about tonality and instrumentation, deal with each separately and try to draw out conclusions. For tonality you could show how keys are defined by cadences in the piece, how the modulations are all to related keys, how the return of the final section is signalled by a section of dominant preparation, and how the ending is marked by a series of perfect cadences in the tonic – remember to give a location for each example you mention. This is far better than just listing events without analysis (e.g. 'It starts in G major, and modulates to D major, B minor, E minor' etc.).

4. Quotations of what other people have written about the music are best avoided. Examiners want to discover what you know about the music, not how well you can memorise quotations.

5. Be concise, avoid repeating yourself and keep to the facts. Words that we often use in speech while the brain ticks over, such as 'actually', 'basically' or 'generally' are seldom necessary in written exam answers.

If you find written English difficult, remember that you can answer the Part B questions in short note form or as a list of bullet points. If you do this, make sure that your meaning is totally clear and unambiguous and remember the importance of giving an example (with location) of each point you make.

In Part C, an essay is essential, but don't dive in too quickly. First check that you have chosen the title about which you feel most confident – you don't want to get halfway into the essay before realising that the other choice would have been better.

Then spend a few minutes planning what to include. If you start without a plan, you are likely to miss points, repeat yourself and

When writing about dates, be careful not to confuse years with centuries. We live in the 21st century, but the years begin with 20, not 21. Similarly, 1750 is in the 18th century, not the 17th century.

fail to deal with matters in a logical order, so a few minutes making a plan is time well spent. It can be quite simple. Let's make a plan for an essay in which you have to compare and contrast rhythm and melody in three works which we will call A (from the Baroque period), B (from the Classical period) and C (a 20th-century work):

1. Introduction. Establish the context by naming the style and/or dates of the three works concerned.

   There is no need to copy out the question or to 'set the scene' with lots of background detail.

2. Body of the essay. Compare and contrast aspects of the rhythm in works A, B and C, and then deal with the melodic writing in the three works.

   It is usually clearer to deal with each element separately in questions of this type. There is no point in simply describing the rhythms and melodies in each work. Concentrate on important features. For example, work A might feature dotted rhythms and hemiolas, work B might have many simple repeated rhythms, while work C might contain unusual metres, changing time signatures and syncopation. Then deal with important aspects of melody in a similar way.

3. End with a conclusion that summarises your main points and that ties in with your opening paragraph.

   Here, we might observe that the dotted rhythms and hemiolas of work A are characteristic of many Baroque pieces, the simple quaver accompaniments supporting a more florid melody in B are typical of the Classical period, and that the irregular metres and rhythms of C are a feature of many early 20th-century works.

Make sure that you practise writing timed essays before the actual exam. Running out of time is a common way of losing marks, so try not to let that happen to you.

Finally, don't apologise! If you get really stuck, remember that you will get no marks for writing something like 'I don't know much about this piece' or 'I was absent when we studied this work'. Nor will you get marks for paraphrasing points that you've already made. Have a go – after all, you will have the score in front of you and careful observation of the music will almost certainly produce some extra marks that you might otherwise have lost.

In the rest of this book we discuss all of the set works for exams in 2013 and 2014. For each year we deal with the instrumental works first, with an exercise after each one so that you can check your understanding of the text. At the end of these sections there are essay questions on comparisons and contrasts between the works, similar in style to those in Section C of the paper. The applied music works are then discussed, again with an exercise after each one, and at the end of these sections there are some sample questions in the style of those you will encounter in Part B of the paper. The glossary at the end of the book can be used to look up the meaning of terms printed in **bold**.

Set works for 2013

If you are taking A2 Music in summer 2013, you have to study the seven pieces of instrumental music *below*, plus the five pieces of applied music in the section starting on page 62.

Instrumental music

The pieces for this area of study span musical periods from the end of the Renaisssance to the late 20th century:

1550	1600	1650	1700	1750	1800	1850	1900	1950	2000
Renaissance		Baroque			Classical		Romantic		Modern

Holborne
NAM 13
1599

Haydn
NAM 16
1781

Brahms
NAM 18
1865

Debussy
NAM 5
1894

Poulenc
NAM 19
1922

Davis
NAM 50
1954

Reich
NAM 12
1985

Pavane 'The image of melancholy' and Galliard 'Ecce quam bonum' (Anthony Holborne)

These two movements were first published in London in 1599, during the reign of Queen Elizabeth I, as part of a large collection of similar pieces by this composer. Little is known about Anthony Holborne, who died in 1602, but as a writer of instrumental music he was highly regarded by his contemporaries.

They are written for five soloists and were probably intended for performance in the home, either for the enjoyment of the players or for a small, educated audience. **Chamber music** of this type was known as consort music in Elizabethan England and was usually played on whatever instruments were available (as indicated in the note printed above the score). Music printing was still relatively new (and expensive) in the late Renaissance and so publishers frequently indicated that pieces could be played on a variety of instruments in order to maximise sales. The parts are not typical of any one particular instrument and are fairly limited in range.

On CD2 Holborne's pieces are played by a consort of viols of different sizes. These were bowed and fretted string instruments, held on the lap or between the knees. A consort of five viols was the most popular medium for the performance of chamber music at this time, but wind instruments (such as a consort of recorders) were also used.

The pavane was a moderately slow courtly dance in duple time, performed by couples in a stately, processional style. In contrast, the galliard was much more energetic and in triple time. The two dances were often paired in Renaissance music. However, while the pavane and galliard in NAM 13 were printed next to each other in the original publication, it is unlikely that they were intended as a matching pair – their keys, instrumental ranges, themes and descriptive titles are all different.

Context and forces

NAM 13 (page 191)	CD2 Tracks 1–2
Rose Consort of Viols	

One of the best ways to get to know NAM 13 is to play or sing it with a group of friends. It will suit various different combinations of performers, as the original publication indicates.

Although Holborne used dance forms for both movements, the dense **counterpoint**, which provides independent melodic interest for all five players, indicates that this is music for the ear rather than the feet.

Holborne added descriptive titles to a number of his dances, often of a seemingly private nature that is now sometimes unclear. Many of these, such as 'The image of melancholy', express sorrow and may reflect the grief of his patron, the Countess of Pembroke, who had lost three close family members in a single year. 'Ecce quam bonum' ('Behold how good a thing it is') is the Latin title of one of the Biblical psalms that the Countess had famously adapted into English rhyming verse and presented to Queen Elizabeth in 1599.

> 'Ecce quam bonum' is also a quotation used by the poet Dante, to whose works Holborne refers in several other of his descriptive titles.

Structure

Like much dance music of the period, both movements consist of three independent sections (at the time known as 'strains'), each of which is repeated. We could summarise this as AA BB CC form. The symmetry of the galliard, in which each strain is eight bars long, with cadences every four bars in sections A and B, reflects the dance style of the movement. However, the sections in the pavane are 16, 17 and 26 bars in length – a degree of irregularity which again suggests that this is not music for actual dancing.

Tonality

The pavane is in D major, with perfect cadences in the tonic at the end of the first and third strains, and in the dominant (A major) at the end of the middle strain. The tonal system of related major and minor keys was only just beginning to emerge in the late Renaissance, but here it is reinforced by a tonic pedal in bars 34–39 and a dominant **pedal** in bars 54–57. However, traces of older modality are evident in **false relations**, such as the G(♮) followed by G♯ in the outer parts of bar 13.

> Today D minor is written with a key signature of one flat, but at this time it was usual to flatten the 6th degree of the minor scale (B♭ in this key) only where needed.

The galliard is in the key of D minor (see *left*). The first and last strains end with perfect cadences in D minor (both including a **tierce de Picardie**), while the second strain ends with a **phrygian cadence** (IVb–V) in the same key.

Melody and rhythm

The pavane starts with a dotted **figure** in the top part that descends by step from tonic to dominant. Holborne's contemporaries would easily have recognised this as a gesture frequently associated with grief in Elizabethan music – compare it with the start of the vocal melody in 'Flow my tears' (NAM 33).

The melodic writing is much like that found in vocal music of the period – mainly **conjunct**, with occasional small leaps. Wider leaps are generally followed by balancing stepwise movement in the opposite direction, as in the top part of the pavane, bars 34–37. The lowest part has more leaps than the others, because it is often providing the bass of chords whose roots are a 4th or a 5th apart.

Holborne captures the elegant style of a pavane through the use of simple minim- and crotchet-based rhythms, enlivened with a little discreet **syncopation** (as in the top part of bar 19).

The lively style of a galliard is conveyed in its first section through the use of dotted rhythms and two different types of syncopation. The first is caused by the off-beat entry of the dotted figure in the fourth voice down and occurs every time this rising figure enters (the second crotchet of bars 2, 5 and 6). The second is caused by temporarily switching from triple to duple metre, although without changing the time signature. There are clearly three minim beats ($\frac{3}{2}$ time) in each of the first two bars, but in bars 3 and 7 the metre changes to two dotted-minim beats, as found in $\frac{6}{4}$ time, emphasised by the change of chord halfway through these bars.

The rhythms in the second and third strains of the galliard are less busy, but are enlivened by the use of **hemiola** in bars 10–11 and 14–15, where the triple pulse becomes, without change of time signature, a count of 1–2, 1–2, 1–2, in each pair of bars. Hemiola is yet another type of syncopation and is characteristic of many triple-time dances written in the Renaissance and Baroque periods.

Texture

The pavane is written in five-part imitative counterpoint. A lack of rests means that the imitation is not always obvious. For example, the opening notes of the top part are imitated one minim later by the fourth part down. At the start of the second section this figure is adapted to make a longer motif, imitated by the second part down in bars 18–19. The third section begins with a scalic figure in the middle part that is an inversion of the initial 'melancholy' motif; it is imitated by all parts except the bass.

Despite an even greater scarcity of rests, the texture of the galliard is more varied, with pervasive imitation in sections A and C, and a largely **homophonic** central section.

Harmony

The majority of chords are root-position or first-inversion triads. Cadences at the end of strains are perfect, except in section B of the galliard, which is imperfect (or, more precisely, **phrygian**). The only on-the-beat discords are **suspensions**, often decorated as they resolve and sometimes overlapped with suspensions in other parts. In the example *right* you can see how the dissonant 7th between the outer parts at bar 4^1 is prepared (P), suspended (S), decorated (D) and resolved (R). As it resolves to C♯ the second part down starts a similar process with a note that is to form a 4th above the bass (regarded as a dissonant interval in Holborne's day) in bar 5.

Be aware that not all tied notes are suspensions: for example, those in bars 1 and 2 of the pavane do not form discords. There are only three suspensions in the galliard: can you find them?

The score

Notice that the third part down has an alto C clef, in which the middle line of the stave represents middle C. The first note of the pavane in this part is therefore A. Also be aware that the parts frequently cross each other: so, for example, the highest notes in bar 41 of the pavane are played by the middle part.

In common with most music of the period, there are no performance directions, not even tempo or dynamic markings. However the performers on CD2 introduce variety by adding ornamentation when each of the sections is repeated, some of which is shown *right*. Decoration of this sort was an important performing convention at the time this music was composed. Can you identify other places where the music is ornamented in the repeats?

Upper three parts (bars 9±10)

Second part (bars 13±15)

Exercise 1

1. What is a false relation? Identify the location of a false relation in bars 17–33 of the pavane.

2. Name the harmonic device used in bars 54–57 of the pavane.

3. In bar 1 of the galliard, how does the music played by the fourth part down relate to the music played by the top part?

4. How does the top part in bar 22 of the galliard relate to the same part in the previous bar?

5. What are the main similarities and differences between the pavane and the galliard?

6. Which features of NAM 13 suggest that this was *not* music intended for actual dancing?

7. Which features of NAM 13 indicate that it dates from the late Renaissance?

String Quartet 'The Joke': movement 4 (Haydn)

Context and forces

NAM 16 (page 202)   CD2 Track 5
The Lindsays

For much of his life Haydn was director of music to the Hungarian Prince Esterházy at a magnificent palace 50 kilometres south-east of Vienna. Here he had musicians at his disposal to supply the court with a huge variety of music, ranging from operas, church music and orchestral works, to intimate pieces of **chamber music** in which the prince himself often took part as one of the performers.

Haydn established the string quartet as the most successful and long-lasting of all **genres** of chamber music. The combination of two violins, viola and cello proved ideal. The instruments blend superbly well and can offer full four-part harmony and a wide variety of textures.

By the time Haydn wrote the movement in NAM 16 he had completed at least 30 string quartets, gradually developing a style in which all four instruments are treated as equally important. He had also settled on a four-movement format, typically in the order fast – slow – minuet – finale. The last of these is usually the fastest of the four movements and is often (as here) cast in the form of a jolly **rondo**, in which a main section alternates with a series of contrasting sections.

In 1781, after Haydn had completed the six quartets published as his opus 33, he wrote to potential purchasers describing them as 'written in a new and special manner'. Although this statement was perhaps just a marketing ploy, the way in which Haydn provides musical interest in all four parts was certainly a feature that would appeal to the increasing number of amateur musicians who were playing string quartets at home, purely for their own pleasure.

These works are also lighter in style than some of Haydn's earlier quartets and often deliberately humorous. NAM 16 is the finale of the second quartet of the set. It is nicknamed *The Joke* for reasons that will become apparent, but all six quartets contain many appealing features, including melodies that are frequently folk-like in their dancing simplicity.

Structure

As in many of Haydn's finales, the form of NAM 16 is a rondo, a structure in which a main section in the tonic, called the **refrain**, alternates with contrasting sections, usually in related keys, called **episodes**. It is unusual in that the refrain gets shorter each time it appears, and that the second episode is in the tonic key. Although we've used the letters A, B and C to show the structure, the themes in these sections are closely related and so sound very similar (the movement could, in fact, be described as **monothematic**).

The refrain (A) has a structure called **rounded binary form** because material from the first section comes round again near the end. Its first section is eight bars long and concludes with a perfect cadence in the tonic, E♭ major. It is repeated. The second section (B, bars 8–28), remains in E♭, but is distinguished from A by:

➤ A slower **harmonic rhythm** at the start (V for two bars, then I for two bars) and a more sustained style of accompaniment

➤ Prominent **appoggiaturas** at the ends of the third and fourth two-bar phrases (bars 14 and 16)

➤ A long dominant **pedal** (bars 16–28) supporting some **chromatic** colouring (A♮ and G♭, both resolving by step, one to the root and the other to the fifth of chord V).

The final bars of B are **dominant preparation** for an exact repeat of A in bars 28–36 (the 'rounding' of the binary form), after which the entire second section is marked to be repeated (see *right*).

The first episode (C, bars 36–70) focuses on A♭ major in bars 36–47 and F minor in bars 48–53, but neither key is established with a root-position tonic chord. Haydn then returns to E♭ major for bars 54–70. The harmonic rhythm speeds up after the last pedal resolves to chord I of E♭ major (bar 59). This progression includes a sequential rise from tonic to submediant (I–IV–II–V–III–VI in bars 59–61), creating tension which is released when VIIb of V (the second chord of bar 63) resolves to another dominant pedal of E♭ major in bars 64–68.

The entire rounded binary structure of the refrain (ABA but without any repeats) then returns in bars 71–107.

The second episode (bars 107–140) is a modified repeat of the first episode, so we'll call it C¹. It stays in the tonic key throughout, and ends with yet another another dominant pedal (bars 128–140).

The final refrain is shorn of its B section. It starts with a repeat of just section A in bars 140–148, but then Haydn surprisingly adds a short Adagio that begins with a melodramatic dominant major 9th (bars 148–149) and ends with another perfect cadence in the tonic key.

Section A returns, but it is now chopped up into its constituent two-bar phrases by silences (see *right*). The perfect cadence in bars 165–166 seems to be the end – Haydn follows it with three bars of silence to tempt a premature round of applause, but he's playing a joke. Suddenly the refrain starts up again! Before the audience has time to work out what's going on, it fizzles out after only two bars – another joke, since this really is the end.

Bars	Section	Key
0–36	‖: A :‖: BA :‖	E♭ major
36–70	C	A♭, Fm, E♭
71–107	ABA	E♭ major
107–140	C¹	E♭ major
140–172	A (Adagio) A¹	E♭ major

G.P. in bar 155 and later stands for General Pause. This indicates that everyone is silent in these bars, not that there is necessarily any pause in the pulse. The figure 3 along with the rests in bar 167 indicates that the last of these general pauses extends through three complete bars.

Nearly all of the thematic material derives from motifs in the opening theme of the refrain. which is underpinned by strongly **functional harmony**:

Harmonic sequence

In the theme itself motif *y* is inverted (*y¹* above) then repeated to form the rising scale in bar 6. In bars 9–13 chromatic notes are added to both motifs, and in bars 22–24 the middle note of motif *x* is shortened to produce playful slurred quavers. This new version of *x* is then repeated to form the chromatic **sequence** in bars 24–27.

Many more manipulations of this material occur throughout the movement – try to spot some for yourself.

The jokes

The nickname for this work should really be 'the jokes' as there is more than one. For example, at bar 16 the cello begins a dominant **pedal** that lasts for 13 bars, creating expectancy for a terrific musical event. What actually follows is the tiny eight-second musical squib of the refrain (bars 28–36).

The central episode begins with another dominant pedal, this time in the key of Ab major (bars 36–47). But instead of resolving to chord I in bar 41 the music gets stuck on chord Ic, not once, but four times. Every time this happens chord Ic is marked *sf* (suddenly accented) as though Haydn were venting his fury at being unable to find the root position. He then moves down to F minor with a similar lack of success (bars 48–53). Having failed to establish either key, Haydn gives up and returns to Eb major and, after two abortive attempts (bars 55 and 57), at last achieves a perfect cadence in bars 58–59. To celebrate his success he uses motif *y* in a rising sequence which leads to … another dominant pedal (bars 64–68)!

By the time we get to the second episode, 54 out of 107 bars have featured prolonged dominant pedals so it is a relief to hear a tonic pedal (bars 107–111) and what sound like some conclusive perfect cadences (bars 120–123). But Haydn hasn't finished – he continues to another dominant pedal (bars 128–141) and some fun with a truncated version of motif *x*. A total silence and melodramatic **appoggiaturas** (bar 139) lead to a dominant 7th (note the pitch of the viola in bar 140). After another dramatic silence that catchy refrain sneaks in yet again.

Could this be the end? No! A loud dominant 9th ushers in the Adagio almost as if we're in for an extra slow movement, just when we thought it was all over. But all movement stops and the wretched refrain starts up yet again. But this time it is in its death throes – chopped into pieces by the general pause that interrupts every two bars. After the silence has expanded to a total of more than four bars (a long time when you are trying not to giggle) Haydn pulls his last rabbit out of the hat in the shape of the first two bars of the movement which, we now discover, already contain the perfect cadence with which the work abruptly ends.

The score

Note that the viola part is in the alto C clef throughout, and that the *sf* accents in bars 41 and 43 are emphasised by **double-stopping** in the first violin part. Notice also that since the time of Holborne, nearly 200 years earlier, composers were adding much more performance detail in their scores, including dynamic and articulation marks (staccatos, slurs and *sforzandi*).

Style

NAM 16 is typical of the Classical style in many of its features. **Periodic phrasing** – pairs of equal-length phrases sounding like questions and answers – is seen in the example printed *opposite*. This also shows the Classical preference for clear harmonic progressions, centred on chords I and V^7, with regular cadences to define keys. Progressions such as $II–V^7–I$ in bars 35–36 are a feature of the style, as are appoggiaturas, both chromatic (B♮ in bar 161) and diatonic (G in bar 165). Finally, the texture of melody-dominated **homophony** (but with plenty of interest in the accompanying parts) is typical of much Classical music.

Exercise 2

1. In harmony, what is a pedal? In which bars does a pedal occur (a) in the viola part, and (b) in the violin 1 part? How, apart from the instrument used, do these two pedals differ?

2. What is double-stopping? Where is it used on page 206 of NAM?

3. What is meant by harmonic rhythm? In what way is the harmonic rhythm in bars 9–28 different from that in the first eight bars?

4. Which note in the first-violin part of bar 5 is chromatic?

5. In a rondo, what is the difference between the refrain and an episode?

6. Explain the precise meaning of the letters G.P. and the figure 3 in bars 167–169.

7. Describe the main way in which the instruments used in the recording of this quartet differ from the instruments used in the recording of the pieces by Holborne in NAM 13.

Piano Quintet in F minor: movement 3 (Brahms)

Context and forces

Brahms was a Romantic composer with a great respect for earlier music. He studied Baroque counterpoint, helped to edit the music of Handel, and wrote variations on themes by Handel and Haydn. Brahms was also strongly influenced by the music of Beethoven, written earlier in the 19th century, especially its intensive use of short motifs and its use of **tonality** to define the structure of large movements. These influences unfairly led some of his contemporaries to dismiss Brahms' music as conservative, but in other respects, such as lyrical melody and rich harmonies, he was as Romantic as most late 19th-century composers.

NAM 18 (page 231)   CD2 Track 7
Guarneri Quartet with Peter Serkin
(piano)

Brahms often revised his compositions before he was satisfied; this work was first written as a string quintet in 1862 then rewritten for piano duet in 1864. NAM 18 is from the third version, published in 1865 for piano quintet (an ensemble of five solo instruments – often, as here, two violins, viola, cello and piano). It is therefore a type of chamber music, like NAM 13 and NAM 16, but on a much larger scale than these earlier works. NAM 18 is just one of four movements in a work with a total length of around 45 minutes.

The work was probably first performed privately, but its scale and difficulty suggest that Brahms intended the work for professional performance in small concert halls, rather than for amateurs to play at home. Brahms certainly intended the work for highly skilled performers: the movement in NAM is fast and technically demanding, and all of the instrumentalists are required to use a wide range, which is particularly evident in bars 146–157.

Structure

NAM 18 consists of a scherzo followed by a trio, after which the scherzo is repeated. This gives the overall movement a **ternary** (ABA) structure.

A scherzo (meaning a joke) was a fast triple-time movement in the Classical period, but Brahms uses both $\frac{6}{8}$ and $\frac{2}{4}$ metres, and his style is much more serious than that found in the light and witty of scherzos of earlier times.

A trio is a middle section of a movement, intended to contrast with the outer parts that surround it. Such sections were once written for just three instruments, hence the name trio.

Scherzo (bars 1–193[1])

First, listen for the three themes of the scherzo, which we will label A, B and C.

A (bars 1–12)

The first is a rising melody in C minor and compound time. It is characterised by frequent syncopations and is *pianissimo*. Brahms' interest in counterpoint is evident at bar 9 where the theme played in octaves by violin and viola is imitated by the piano.

B (bars 13–21)

The second is a jerky melody (staccato notes separated by tiny rests) also in C minor but in simple time. It revolves obsessively around the dominant and is also played *pianissimo*.

C (bars 22–37)

The third is a very loud march-like theme in C major with strong second-beat accents (marked *forzando*). Although this sounds very different in mood, it is closely integrated with the previous section because the motif in bars 22–24 is an **augmentation** of the semiquaver figure in bar 14, but now an octave higher, and in C major rather than C minor:

This theme is immediately repeated at bar 30, where Brahms adds variety by using the piano to imitate the strings two beats later (starting at the $f\!f$ in bar 31).

There are then varied repeats of A (bars 38–56) and B (bars 57–67), modulating rapidly in the process. This leads to the distant key of E♭ minor and the central section of the scherzo, in which counterpoint becomes the most important element.

Brahms uses a **fugal** texture in which the viola treats the first four bars of theme B as a fugue subject (bar 67). This is answered by the piano (right hand, bar 71). There are further entries of the subject starting in bars 76 (violin 1) and 84 (viola). These are combined with no fewer than three countersubjects (themes that are played simultaneously with the subject), introduced as follows:

**Fugato
(bars 67–100)**

1. Piano left hand, bar 67 (next heard in viola, bar 71)
2. Piano left hand, bar 71 (next heard in viola, bar 76)
3. Viola, bar 80 (next heard modified by violin 2, bar 84).

In bars 88–100 all of these melodies are fragmented into tiny cells in a complex five-part contrapuntal texture. The example *below* shows how, in the first-violin part, ten notes of the subject are detached *(a)*, then just five notes *(b)*, then three notes *(c)*. Notice how the pitches rise sequentially until the climax at bar 100.

Comparing this example with the examples of fragmentation at the foot of page 18 will help show how Brahms was often indebted to Beethoven in the compositional processes he used.

Can you spot similar processes at work in the cello and piano parts of bars 88–100 of the quintet? These fragments (and those of the viola from bar 92) are heard in a type of close imitation known as **stretto**.

The fragment marked *x* in the example *above* is a motif that will recur in various transformations, imparting a sense of unity to the structure.

After this central section Brahms repeats the themes of the first part (A, B and C) but in the following order:

B (bars 100–109): E♭ minor
C (bars 109–124): E♭ major (the relative major of C minor)
A (bars 125–157): E♭ minor modulating to C minor
B (bars 158–193): C minor (greatly extended to form a **coda** and with a **tierce de Picardie** in the C major chord at the end).

Shown *right* are just two of Brahms' transformations of motif *x*. The first is an **augmentation** of *x* (every note is four times longer than before). The second is in E♭ major instead of E♭ minor and an ornament has been added to its fifth beat (at *y*).

The entire work is unified by devices of this sort. The falling semitone that constantly appears in the final bars of the example *above* is heard prominently throughout the scherzo. Even the contrasting trio is linked with the scherzo by several common motifs, the most obvious being motif *y* (*right*) which becomes an integral part of its main melody (bars 197 and 199).

Violin 2 (bars 105±108)

Violin 1 (bars 109±112)

**Trio
(bars 193²–261)**

Not only is the entire movement in ternary form, but its middle section (the trio) also has a ternary structure:

A   Bars 193–225: This section begins with a broad 16-bar melody in C major that modulates to B major in the last five bars. It is introduced by piano and then repeated by strings, and strongly contrasts with the episodic nature and contrapuntal textures of the scherzo.

B   Bars 225–241: Legato melody with staccato bass; in bars 233–241 these parts are then reversed – melody in the bass with staccato accompaniment above. The harmony is chromatic but anchored to C major by a dominant pedal (on G) whose triplets form **cross-rhythms** against the quavers in the other parts.

A   Bars 242–261: The first 11 bars of the melody from the first section return, in a dark texture in which all instruments are in a low **tessitura**. This leads to a **plagal cadence** in C (bars 253–254) and a tonic pedal (bars 254–261).

The performers are then instructed to repeat the scherzo – *Scherzo da Capo sin al Fine* is Italian for repeat the scherzo as far as the word *Fine* (the end).

Other points

Apart from the bold, rising theme at the start, Brahms' melodic material is based mainly on motifs of a narrow range which are manipulated in many different ways, as we have seen. His textures are equally varied, ranging from the **monophonic** opening to the **fugal** texture starting in bar 67. Question 4 in the next exercise invites you to identify some other textures for yourself.

One of the hallmarks of the Romantic style is the use of chromatic harmony. Even in the first phrase Brahms gradually builds up the notes of an **augmented-6th chord** (A♭–C–E♭–F♯) that resolves to chord V in the second half of bar 6 over a continuing tonic pedal in the cello part. Pedal points also play an important role in the trio, which begins and ends over a tonic pedal on C (bars 194–201 and 249²–261). The chromatic writing of its entire central section (bars 226–241) is underpinned by a dominant pedal on G, which starts in the piano and then transfers to the cello in bar 233.

But occasionally, Brahms' interest in early music seems to surface. For example, the root-position triads in bars 18–21 are given a modal colour by the minor version of chord V (bar 19²), and he ends this section on a chord without a 3rd (G and D in bar 21) – a feature often found in early music.

Brahms' preference for the dark sound of E♭ minor as a secondary key, rather than the simple relative major of C minor (E♭ major) introduces a more complex type of tonal relationship than we saw in the movement by Haydn, much of which remains rooted in the tonic key. However, Brahms reinforces each key in NAM 18 with clear cadences, and the pedal points also help to define the tonal structure. Notice that most sections end with an imperfect cadence to project the music forward, rather than with a decisive perfect cadence to punctuate the onward flow.

Exercise 3

1. What in the music suggests that this movement was written to be played by professional performers in the concert hall rather than by amateurs at home?

2. Describe some of the ways in which the main themes of the scherzo (up to bar 193) are contrasted.

3. In bars 18^2–20^1 the first violinist is required to use **double-stopping**. What does this mean?

4. Use an appropriate word or phrase to describe the texture in each of the following passages:
    (i)   bars 15–17
    (ii)   bars 57–59
    (iii)   bars 88–94.

5. Name the harmonic device used in the bass part of bars 53–56.

6. What is the meaning of 8va ------------¬ above the first violin part in bars 61–66?

7. What does the term countersubject mean?

8. What happens if the rhythm of a motif is augmented?

9. How is the trio contrasted with the scherzo?

10. This movement is in the key of C minor, but it ends at bar 193 on a *tierce de Picardie*. Explain what is meant by a *tierce de Picardie* and name the chord that it forms in the key of C minor.

Prélude à L'Après-midi d'un faune (Debussy)

The first three pieces we studied were all types of chamber music, written for small groups of soloists. Debussy's 'Prelude to the Afternoon of a Faun' is written for orchestra and is a type of orchestral music known as a tone poem – a work in which music is used to reflect the content of a story, poem, painting or scene. Debussy described this piece as a prelude because he originally intended to follow it with two further movements – a plan later abandoned. It is now usually played as a short concert work, although it has also been used as ballet music.

The *Prélude* was first performed in Paris in 1894 and it evokes images from a poem by the French writer Stéphane Mallarmé about a faun – an ancient nature-god, half goat and half man – who awakes in the shimmering heat of a summer afternoon and languidly plays his panpipes while watching two water nymphs. His passion aroused, the faun seizes the nymphs, but they are frightened by his burning kisses and the vision vanishes. As night falls he stretches himself voluptuously on the sand to sleep, imagining in an erotic dream that he now possesses the nymphs.

The fluidity of Debussy's music, and the sensual harmonies he used to convey the sultry images of the poem, quickly marked out the work as far in advance of its time, looking forward to some of the new directions music was to take in the 20th century.

Context and genre

NAM 5 (page 86)   CD1 Track 5
Concertgebouw Orchestra
Conducted by Bernard Haitink

Form

Bars		Subsections	
1–54	**A**	1–30	A¹
		31–36	Transition
		37–54	A²
55–78	**B**	Melody played 3 times:	
		woodwind (55–62)	
		upper strings (63–74)	
		solo violin (75–78)	
79–93	**A**	79–93	Recap of A¹ only
		94–110	Coda

The structure of NAM 5 is as deliberately ambiguous as its keys and its harmonies, so there are many different accounts of the work. However, we can say that it is in **ternary form** (shown *left*) in which the A sections are in sharp keys (centred on E major) and the B section is in flat keys (centred on D♭ major).

Listen to the music and make sure that you can recognise the main ideas. Try to decide what you feel are the most important features of the music and see if you agree that they include:

➤ Complex rhythms that disguise a regular pulse

➤ Melodic variation (rather than *development* of motifs)

➤ Rich colourful harmony that often seems to obscure the keys of the music rather than define them

➤ Subtle orchestral textures.

Style

All of these features contribute to a style of music in which the atmosphere created by colour, tone and texture seems more important than clearly-defined phrases and structures. This late Romantic style, which looks forward to some features of 20th-century music, is known as **impressionism**. The term is borrowed from French painting of the period in which there is a similar interest in conveying the impression of light and movement, rather than giving an exact representation of shapes.

Melody

The unaccompanied flute melody at the start is among the most famous passages in all music. It represents the panpipes played by the faun in the drowsy heat of afternoon, timeless and still. Debussy does this through:

➤ Fluid rhythms that lack any sense of time-bound metre

➤ Pitches which avoid a sense of tonality by swinging chromatically through the **tritone** between C♯ and G♮ (see *left*)

➤ An inconclusive ending on A♯, which is not one of the main notes of any key suggested by the key signature.

It is difficult to imagine anything further removed from the tightly engineered motifs of NAM 18, written only 30 years earlier by Brahms. Nor is there any similarity if we examine how Debussy later uses this opening flute melody:

➤ He repeats it unchanged with an accompaniment of fluttering **tremolo** strings (bars 11–14)

➤ He lengthens the first note and decorates the melody of bar 3 with demi-semiquaver triplets (bars 21–22)

➤ He ends a phrase with a fast version of the first bar (bars 26–27)

➤ He slows the whole melody down (bars 79–82 and 86–89) …

and so on. At no point is there a sense of motifs being developed in the way that we saw in the works by Haydn and Brahms. Instead, Debussy presents the same theme in various rhythmic and melodic variants, and in different textures and harmonisations.

The key of the work is E major, but there is little clue of this in the chromatic opening, and the first chord in NAM 5, heard in bar 4, is the exotic discord shown right – a half-diminished 7th on A♯ (which could alternatively be described as a chord of C♯ minor with an added 6th – see *right*).

Just as important is what happens immediately after this chord. The G♯ and A♯, now notated as A♭ and B♭, are repeated in bar 5 while the other two notes of the half-diminished 7th (C♯ and E) rise a semitone to D and F, the four notes forming a chord of B♭⁷. Nothing could be further from the key of E major, and the effect is like a curtain rising to reveal a whole new tonal world.

In conventional harmony, B♭⁷ is the dominant seventh of E♭ major, but here it is drained of any dominant function by its context, for, after a bar of total silence (bar 6), C♯m^add.6 returns on divided and muted strings, only to be followed once more by B♭⁷, now decorated with fragmentary horn motifs (bars 7–10). When the flute melody returns in bar 11 it is harmonised with a major 7th on D, a chord related to B♭⁷ only by a single common note (D).

It is these successions (not progressions) of unrelated discords that prompted the composer Boulez to suggest that the *Prélude à L'Après-midi d'un faune* was 'the beginning of modern music'. A tonal progression suggests purposeful motion from and towards a defined goal (the tonic). Debussy's succession of chords is simply a series of harmonic colours suspended out of time.

Other characteristic features of Debussy's elusive approach to tonality and harmony can be seen in:

➤ Bars 33 and 34, where the clarinet and flute parts rise and fall through **whole-tone scales**

➤ Bar 37, where the use of **parallel chords** (B⁷–D♯⁷–C♯⁷) is clear in the accompanying crotchets.

The middle section (bars 55–78) is differentiated by its key, which is unrelated to the first section (in fact, D♭ major is about as far from E major as it is possible to get). However, when the opening A section returns, the rhythmically **augmented** variant of the original flute melody (bars 79–83) is accompanied by an unambiguous chord of E major in first inversion, at last making the home key clearer – although only briefly, as Debussy then slips through C major (bars 83–85) and E♭ major (bars 86–89). The section from bar 94 to the end can be regarded as a **coda** and here, at last, the tonic key of E major is no more in doubt.

A further taste of Debussy's harmonic style can be seen in the final perfect cadence (shown *right*). There is little tonal tension – the cadence seems to be enveloped in a haze of sound. This is partly attributable to the fact that the leading note (D♯) puts in a late and very quiet appearance in the dominant chord, and partly by the diatonic discords (7ths, 9ths, 11ths and 13ths above the dominant) that add sensuous colour rather than tonal direction. Debussy goes out of his way to ensure that a regular pulse will not be apparent by introducing lazy duplets and groups of four, completely disguising the compound-time beat as the music drifts timelessly to its close.

Tonality and harmony

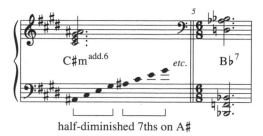

half-diminished 7ths on A♯

E major: V¹³   V⁹   V⁹   I

Orchestration

When following the score, note that:

➢ The cor anglais (a deep-sounding oboe) and the horns in F sound a perfect 5th lower than written

➢ Clarinets in A sound a minor 3rd lower than written (in the middle section the players are instructed to use clarinets in B♭, which sound a tone lower than written)

➢ Double basses sound an octave lower than written

➢ Antique cymbals are metal discs, about 4 inches in diameter, that produce a bell-like tone which sounds two octaves higher than written.

Viola parts are, as normal, written in the alto C clef (in which the middle line represents middle C) and Debussy uses the tenor C clef (in which the second line from the top represents middle C) for the highest bassoon and cello notes.

The harp parts include instructions on how to set the pitches of the strings (as in bar 1), which is done using the instrument's seven pedals. The term **glissando** tells the player to run the fingertips across the strings – notice how, in bar 4 for example, Debussy tells the player to set the pitches in such a way that this creates a chord (the half-diminished 7th) rather than a scale.

Special instrumental effects in the string parts include *sourdine* – a direction to play with a mute (e.g. bar 5) – and the instruction to play *sur la touche* (e.g. bar 11). This requires the players to bow over the fingerboard, further from the bridge than normal, which creates a gentle, veiled sound. Debussy combines this with a bowed **tremolo** (indicated by the beams through the note stems), which involves short, rapid bow movements causing each note to be rapidly repeated many times, creating a rustling effect.

The importance of instrumental colour to Debussy is apparent in the very first bar, which features the distinctive tone of the flute's lowest **register**. These notes are very quiet so Debussy leaves the melody unobscured by any accompaniment. The tone colour then changes to that of soft horns, with delicate harp glissando and muted string accompaniment.

The middle section of the work is differentiated by the use of sumptuous octave doubling in both wind and strings, as opposed to the soloistic textures of the first section.

The word *cuivré* in bar 92 of the first horn part is a direction for the player to accent the note with a particularly 'brassy' tone.

The music of the last five bars contain many examples of instrumental subtlety. Muted strings are divided into 12 parts to play the tonic chord in bar 106, but the two top notes are played by unmuted solo violins. Muted horns subtly colour the middle range and against this chord two harps play the four-quaver groups. In bar 107 two solo muted horns in 3rds are accompanied by muted first violins for the chromatic fragment from the opening motif of the work. In bar 108 the flute adds a 6th to the tonic chord (echoed by a harp **harmonic**), while the violins play an **appoggiatura** (A♯) that lasts six beats before it resolves. The tiny antique cymbals sound the root and 5th of the tonic chord and almost inaudible pizzicato cellos and basses bring the work to an end.

Exercise 4

1.   What is meant by a tone poem?

2.   In which year, and in which city, was this work first performed?

3.   Why is the tonality ambiguous in the first 20 bars of NAM 5?

4.   Which are the only brass instruments used by Debussy in this work?

5.   What do you notice about the performing directions in this piece compared with NAM 13?

6.   The circles over the last four harp notes indicate the use of harmonics. What does this term mean?

7.   Why is the style of NAM 5 often described as impressionist?

Sonata for Horn, Trumpet and Trombone (Poulenc)

Context

Francis Poulenc was a 20th-century French composer who achieved considerable success in areas as diverse as music for stage and film, church music, songs and chamber music. The last of these includes a number of sonatas and other works for wind instruments, of which NAM 19 (the first movement of a three-movement work) is among the first.

| NAM 19 (page 242) | CD2 Track 8 |
| Nash Ensemble | |

It was written in 1922 and first performed on 4 January 1923 at a concert of contemporary French music in Paris. The work was published in 1924, but Poulenc subsequently produced a revised version in 1945. The technical difficulty of the parts indicates that this is concert music for professional performers.

Style

Much of Poulenc's early music is light and witty, like that of the other five young French composers in a group dubbed *Les Six* by a critic in 1920 (Auric, composer of NAM 42, was another of the group). They disliked the influence that the nostalgic styles of previous generations were having on contemporary music and sought a new clarity and simplicity in their own work. This they found in the **Neoclassical** style that Stravinsky had begun to explore in his ballet *Pulcinella* (NAM 7), completed in 1920.

Combining features of 18th-century music with more modern ideas, the Neoclassical style in NAM 19 is evident in:

➤   Simple diatonic melodies (the opening trumpet theme)

➤   Syncopation (bars 13–14)

➤   Tonal harmonies (chords I, IV and V in bars 1–4)

➤   Discords that spice-up conventional progressions (see *right*)

➤   Humour, in short-winded phrases that constantly change metre and tempo

The recording on CD2 brings out the humour particularly well – listen to how the brass make a headlong dash towards this cadence in bar 4.

➤   Quasi-Classical periodic phrasing (bars 1–4 end with a perfect cadence in the tonic and are answered by bars 5–8 which end with a perfect cadence in the dominant).

However, the piece cannot be mistaken for Classical music. The first cadence includes a 'wrong note' and the second ends in the wrong place (on the weak fourth beat of bar 8). The frequent changes of metre and speed, and the surprising changes of key are nothing like Classical music – nor could an 18th-century trumpet or horn play music of this kind.

Poulenc noted that the audience at the first performance were amazed, and greeted the work with a huge roar of laughter – just the reaction that the composers of *Les Six* hoped for in their early works, which were usually intended to be as deliberately provocative as the art works of the Dada movement (see *left*) that flourished at this time.

Parody was a significant part of the Neo Classical style and so we should seek out the object of Poulenc's good-humoured parodies. Who do you think wrote this melody?

If you gave the name of one composer you are wrong, for the first 11 notes come from NAM 19 (trumpet, bars 2–3) but the remainder come from the first movement of Haydn's String Quartet Op. 71, No. 1 of 1793 (first violin, bars 8–10, transposed to G major).

It is of course Haydn who is the first target for Poulenc's wit. Now compare the first violin part below (which comes from the same movement by Haydn) with Poulenc's trumpet part in bars 0–2³:

Can you see that they begin with the same descending triad (D–B–G) and that they both leap up an octave? Of course, such triadic melodies are two-a-penny in classical music, which is why the trumpet melody at the start of NAM 19 sounds so familiar.

So in what sense is Poulenc's music a parody of classical style? The answer lies in the deliberate banality of Poulenc's three statements of exactly the same motif. Like a bad-tempered teacher, Poulenc's music seems to say 'If I've told you once, I've told you *three times* that the first five notes make a motif that you will jolly well remember for the rest of the movement'. And at the end of the whole phrase (*f très sec*) the brutal detached crotchets proclaim 'this is a cadence at the end of a four-bar phrase – *and don't you forget it*'.

Now look at Haydn's four-bar phrase *above*. The descending triad is heard only once, and the phrase concludes with a simple but highly effective manipulation, so that the end gracefully mirrors the beginning (also compare the second violin part in bar 1 with the first violin part in bar 4). The parallel 6ths in bars 2–4 of this extract are typical, not just of Haydn's music, but of Classical styles in general. The trumpet and horn parts in bars 9–17 of NAM 19 are also in parallel 6ths, but they go on far too long to have come from the pen of a classical composer.

Remember that a horn in F sounds a perfect 5th lower than written. So its first note in bar 9 is E, a 6th below the trumpet's C.

Poulenc's choice of a horn, trumpet and trombone as his trio was highly unusual, and he admitted that it caused him problems of balance. Notice how he addresses this in bar 30 with detailed instructions and differentiated dynamics. Music for brass ensemble is usually written for at least a quartet of instruments, to avoid chords being incomplete and to give each player a chance for an occasional rest while the others continue. With a trio, all three players have to be used almost constantly, apart from where a few very brief unaccompanied solos provide a short break for the other two parts.

The texture mainly consists of melody-dominated **homophony** with some exchange of parts (compare the trumpet in bars 34–35 with the horn in bars 30–31). The tune is often in the trumpet part, but the horn takes the lead in bars 30–33 and 40–47, and becomes the bass instrument in bars 74–81.

This is yet another movement in **ternary form** – an outline of the structure is shown *right*. The opening trumpet figure, based on the tonic triad of G, is bold and **diatonic**, and it forms the start of two balancing four-bar phrases that modulate to the dominant (D major). Shorter phrases, at a quicker tempo and with changing time signatures follow. The trumpet announces a new two-bar idea, starting on the last quaver of bar 17, but the answer to this phrase is the same tune played an octave lower and it slows to a halt in bar 21, just as quickly as it began.

The opening triadic figure returns in bars 21^4–25, but it too has lost all its energy (and its accompaniment), and even its shape, as it fragments among the trio. The horn gets the rhythm of the first two notes 'wrong' (quavers instead of semiquavers) and the trombone slows it down further by augmenting this rhythm to crotchets. The trio then try it more quietly in G minor. Exasperated, they give up further development for the moment and instead embark on the middle section of the ternary structure.

The contrast of key and speed at bar 26 is supported by quiet dynamics and legato phrasing, but this mood is suddenly disrupted by the loud outburst and wild trumpet leaps in bars 36–38. A downward scale for trumpet in free time leads to a dramatic pause, followed by a fast and staccato variation on the opening melody of the movement. This is now played by the horn, with 'oom-pah' accompaniment, but Poulenc retains the pattern of two **balanced phrases**, ending in F major in bar 47. A succession of shorter phrases brings the B section to an end with an unaccompanied downward scale for trumpet. This is repeated in sequence by the horn, ending on D, the dominant of G, ready for the return of G major and a varied repeat of the first section of the movement.

Poulenc begins this with the first eight-bar phrase (bars 57^4–65^4) but he then interpolates material from the B section (bars 65^5–71^3 are taken from bars 47^4–53^3). He then continues with the rest of the A section (bars 73–85, which are taken from bars 9–21). Both of these last two passages are transposed, re-scored and re-harmonised. The **coda** (bars 86–89) consists of an obstinate minor 3rd (B♭) against a *très discret* (very unobtrusive) chromatic scale, followed by a cheeky reference to the opening notes of the movement.

Forces and texture

Structure

Bars		
1–25	A	G major (modulating to the dominant and back)
26–57	B	Mainly in B♭ major (at first slow, but fast from the last quaver of bar 39, where the melody refers back to that of section A)
57^4–89	A¹	G major (varied repeat of section A with a reference to section B in bars 65–72 and a short coda in 86–89)

Exercise 5

1. Check that you understand all the directions in French (translations are on page 537 of NAM).

2. Which of the three instruments in the trio has the *smallest* share of the melodic material?

3. What term describes the texture of bars 22–25? How would you describe the texture in most of the rest of this movement?

4. What sort of scale is heard in the trombone part of bars 86–87?

5. What are the *sounding* pitches of the last three notes played by the horn? Describe the texture of the music in this last bar.

6. What is unusual about Poulenc's use of ternary form in this movement?

7. Explain the meaning of Neoclassical and briefly indicate which aspects of NAM 19 refer to older styles of music and which are clearly 20th century.

Four (opening) (performed by Miles Davis)

Context

Later in the same year that Poulenc's Sonata for Horn, Trumpet and Trombone was first performed (1923), another member of *Les Six* caused a typically Dada-like scandal with his new ballet score, *La création du monde*. The reason for the scandal? Milhaud had based his musical style on the latest rage of the day – jazz.

NAM 50 (page 468)   CD4 Track 9
The Miles Davis Quintet

Jazz had first become widely known through the dixieland style of the early 20th century. This was followed by swing in the 1930s, which became the main type of popular music to be heard in dance halls. However, the essence of jazz is improvisation, and this became increasingly impractical in the 'big bands' that were required to fill the increasingly large halls of the age with regularly-phrased music suitable for dancing.

By the early 1940s some jazz musicians were finding swing too limiting, and they developed a new style called bebop or simply bop. Played by a small combination of musicians (known in jazz as a 'combo'), bebop was music for listening rather than dancing. Its main features can all be heard in *Four* (which dates from 1954):

➢ Fast, driving rhythms

➢ Fragmented melodies with phrases of irregular lengths

➢ Complex, dissonant harmonies

➢ Much solo improvisation, accompanied by a rhythm section of piano, bass and drums.

Gramophone records were limited to just a few minutes of continuous music until the invention of the LP (long-playing) vinyl record in 1948. The LP, offering some 20 minutes of playing time per side, enabled jazz musicians from the 1950s onwards to record the much longer structures they were used to improvising in live performances.

Four was first recorded by the Miles Davis Quartet in 1954 in a version for four players (hence the title) which lacks the saxophone **doubling** heard in the first main section of NAM 50. Track 9 on CD4 contains the first two minutes from a much later recording made at a live concert in New York in 1964, when the complete improvisation lasted six minutes. On other occasions Davis recorded extended versions of the work that could last as long as

15 minutes. So NAM 50 doesn't represent a definitive version of *Four* – it is simply the way in which Davis felt moved to interpret the opening of the piece on the evening of 12 February 1964.

Structure

Four is an example of a **head arrangement** – a term used in jazz for improvised variations on a melody and/or chord progression that the players memorise (keep in the head). The head in *Four* was composed for Miles Davis by the jazz saxophonist Eddie Vinson.

After the drum introduction the 32-bar head is heard for the first time, notated as a 16-bar repeated section (with different first- and second-time endings). Above this, the melody has an ABAB structure (H1 and H9 refer to the boxes in the score):

A (H1) An opening four-bar phrase which is repeated in sequence a 5th lower

B (H9) A contrasting eight-bar idea

A (H1) The first eight bars are repeated

B (H9) The contrasting eight bars are repeated with a different ending that includes a two-bar **break** (solo).

The head is then heard, with some variations, three more times above which Miles Davis improvises the trumpet part. Each of these repetitions is known in jazz as a **chorus**, and in NAM 50 all 32 bars of each chorus are written out in full rather than with the use of repeat signs. The extract ends just after the start of a fourth chorus.

> It is important to realise that NAM 50 is a **transcription**, made by listening to the recording and writing down what is heard. The score doesn't include every detail of each part.

Instruments and textures

The tenor saxophone has no independent material and plays only in the head, where it simply doubles the trumpet an octave lower. This is because the work was originally a quartet (and essentially remains so here), although it also indicates that the head was a composed element, even though the choruses are improvised.

The type of piano playing in the extract is known as **comping** – a jazz term derived from 'accompanying' and indicating a chordal, non-melodic style of accompaniment. The part is rhythmically varied – often syncopated and staccato – but it doesn't have a solo role in this excerpt, which is essentially a showcase for the trumpet-playing talents of Miles Davis. If you compare the piano chords in the head with the basic harmonies printed over the trumpet stave, you will see how musicians in cool jazz freely add 'upper extensions' (9ths, 11ths and 13ths) to triads and 7th chords, as well as embroidering basic progressions with chromatic notes and additional chords.

> The $\triangle$ symbol in some of the chord labels above the piano part indicates that the chord includes a major 7th above the root.

The bass part is played **pizzicato** on a double bass. After the composed head it maintains a **walking bass** pattern that elaborates the harmonies of the head. Occasionally the bassist explicitly outlines the harmony with a simple broken-chord pattern, such as the G-minor triad in bars 1.9–1.10², but more commonly harmony notes are filled in with passing notes and other forms of melodic decoration to produce a more conjunct line. Like Miles Davis, the bassist focuses on higher chord extensions rather than the chord itself, as in bar 1.8, where E♭ is the 9th, and B♭ the minor 13th, of D♭⁷ – he entirely avoids the root and 3rd of the chord in this bar.

He also occasionally plays entirely 'away from the chord', as in bar 1.4 where the notes are a semitone below, and a tone and semitone above, the root of the chord – the root itself is avoided.

The drummer sets the tempo in his introductory solo, after which he plays a supportive role, maintaining a steady beat (played with sticks on a ride cymbal), and punctuating melodic phrases with short **fills** and **rim shots** on the snare drum.

> A rim shot is an accented note produced by striking the rim and the head of the snare drum simultaneously with the same stick, or by positioning one stick with its tip on the drum head and its shaft on the rim, and then striking it with the other stick.

Miles Davis uses a range of what have become known as extended instrumental techniques in his trumpet playing, including:

➢ A deliberately split note (the second note in bar H31, two bars before the start of the first chorus)

➢ A short downward slide called a fall-off (shown by the wavy line in bar 1.15)

➢ **Pitch bend** (bars 1.19–1.20)

➢ A ghost note (the bracketed note in bar 2.1) – a deliberately weak, almost inaudible note

➢ A quarter tone (half of a semitone, indicated by the ♮ sign in bar 2.31)

➢ Half-valving (partially opening a valve to produce a note of thin tone and uncertain pitch, indicated by '½v.' and the diamond-shaped notes in bar 3.32, and in this case having the effect of ornamenting the main note).

Apart from the introductory drum solo and the short trumpet break that leads into the first chorus, the texture of *Four* is melody-dominated homophony, with the tune in the trumpet part and an accompaniment provided by a walking bass part, piano chords and drum rhythms. Variety is provided by the doubling of the melody at the lower octave by tenor saxophone during the head, and by occasional changes in the **tessitura** of the parts, such as the high bass part (indicated by an ottava sign) starting in bar 1.21 and the very high trumpet part at the start of the third chorus.

Harmony and tonality

Four is in E♭ major throughout and its underlying chord sequence, which is more clearly seen in the choruses than in the head, is shown in the shaded row below (added notes and chromatic notes are omitted). The other rows show the actual chords used in each of the three choruses, although the musicians frequently elaborate these harmonies by playing away from the chord:

Bar numbers	1 17	2 18	3 19	4 20	5 21	6 22	7 23	8 24	9 25	10 26	11 27	12 28	13 29	14 30	15 31	16 32
E♭ major	I			IV	ii		IV	♭vii	iii		ii	V	iii		ii	V
Chorus 1	E♭		E♭m⁷	A♭⁷	Fm⁷		A♭m⁷	D♭⁷	Gm⁷		Fm⁷	B♭⁷	Gm⁷		Fm⁷	B♭⁷
	E♭		E♭m⁷	A♭⁷	Fm⁷		A♭m⁷	D♭⁷	E♭	C⁷	Fm⁷	B♭⁷	E♭	B♭⁷	E♭	B♭⁷
Chorus 2	E♭		E♭m⁷		Fm⁷		A♭m⁷		Gm⁷		Fm⁷	B♭⁷	Gm⁷		Fm⁷	B♭⁷
	E♭		E♭m⁷		Fm⁷		A♭m⁷		E♭	C⁷	Fm⁷	B♭⁷	E♭	B♭⁷	E♭	B♭⁷
Chorus 3	E♭		E♭m⁷	A♭⁷	Fm⁷				E♭		Fm⁷	B♭⁷	E♭		Fm⁷	B♭⁷
	E♭		E♭m⁷		Fm⁷		A♭m⁷	D♭⁷	E♭		Fm⁷	B♭⁷	E♭		Fm⁷	B♭⁷

We can see from this table that every 16-bar section:

➤ Begins with two bars of chord I and then moves to the minor form of chord I (with added 7th) in the third bar

➤ Uses chord ii⁷ at the start of its second four-bar phrase (bars 5–6 and 21–22 of each chorus)

➤ Contains the progression ii⁷–V⁷ at the end of its third four-bar phrase (bars 11–12 and 27–28 of each chorus)

➤ Concludes with either ii⁷–V⁷ (bars 15–16) or I–V⁷ (bars 31–32). This is known in jazz as a **turnaround** – a chord progression, designed to lead back to the start by ending on chord V⁷.

But as well as similarities there are differences:

➤ Instead of a change of harmony the previous chord may continue (for example, bars 4, 8, 20 and 24 in chorus 2)

➤ Sometimes an extra chord is added, as in bar 26 of choruses 1 and 2. This chord (C⁷) is a **secondary dominant** of chord ii (Fm) in the key of E♭ major and it launches a route back to E♭ by way of a **circle-of-5ths** progression (C⁷–Fm⁷–B♭⁷–E♭ in bars 26–29)

➤ A chord is sometimes changed to one that has a similar tonal function. This is known as a **substitution chord** in jazz. For example, in the head (see *below*) A♭m⁷ is played in bar 7 and D♭⁷ in bar 8. However, as shown in the table *opposite*, Fm⁷ is substituted for both these chords in the third chorus.

> We say that chords have a similar tonal function if one can replace the other in a progression. For example, viib might be used instead of V⁷ in a perfect cadence, or ii might be used instead of IV as an approach chord to a cadence.

Now look at the chord symbols printed above the trumpet stave in the head. They are summarised in the next table:

Bar numbers	1 / 17	2 / 18	3 / 19	4 / 20	5 / 21	6 / 22	7 / 23	8 / 24	9 / 25	10 / 26	11 / 27	12 / 28	13 / 29	14 / 30	15 / 31	16 / 32
E♭ major	I			IV	ii		IV	♭vii	iii		ii	V	iii		ii	V
Head (1)	E♭		E♭m⁷	A♭⁷	Fm⁷		A♭m⁷	D♭⁷	Gm⁷	F♯m⁷ B⁷	Fm⁷	B♭⁷	Gm⁷	F♯m⁷ B⁷	Fm⁷	B♭⁷
Head (2)	E♭		E♭m⁷	A♭⁷	Fm⁷		A♭m⁷	D♭⁷	Gm⁷	F♯m⁷ B⁷	Fm⁷	B♭⁷	Gm⁷ F♯m⁷ B⁷	Fm⁷ B♭⁷	E♭	

If you compare these chords with those in the table *opposite* you can see that while this is the same chord sequence on which the choruses are based, there are two important differences:

➤ Bars 10, 14 and 26 each contain two chords which form the progression F♯m⁷–B⁷. Although unexpected in E♭ major, in each case F♯m⁷ occurs between Gm⁷ in the previous bar and Fm⁷ in the next bar, forming a chromatic descent to which B⁷ adds the type of additional colour typical of modern jazz

➤ The entire chord progression in bars 13–16 (the four 'first time' bars) is condensed into just two bars on the repeat (bars 29–30). This allows tonic harmony (E♭) to replace the turnaround for the short solo break in bars 31–32.

Both of these features are omitted in the choruses, leaving a slightly simpler harmonic framework as the basis for the improvisation, but this framework is itself subjected to much embellishment, since harmonic complexity is at the heart of bebop.

Let's examine some of the reasons why the harmony is complex in modern jazz. First look at bar H9. The chord shown above the trumpet stave is Gm⁷. The pianist plays this chord in his left hand, and most of the trumpet and bass notes are from the same chord, but on the last quaver of the bar, the pianist plays a chord of F#m⁷. In fact, this is an anticipation (sometimes called a 'push' in jazz) of the chord at the start of the *next* bar, which is indeed F#m⁷. Similar examples of anticipating chords can be seen at the ends of bars H10, H13 and H16.

Many of the more complex chords are formed by extending triads with additional 3rds. For example, the chord in the second half of bar H10 is B¹³. The example *left* shows how this consists of a series of 3rds above B. Notice that the pianist actually plays only the extensions of this chord – and he then goes on to anticipate Fm on the last quaver of the bar.

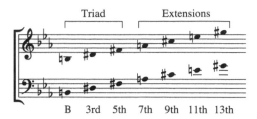

Triad   Extensions

B   3rd 5th 7th 9th 11th 13th

Much of the dissonance typical of bebop also arises from the technique of playing away from the chord – in other words, playing non-chord notes. We have already noted how the bassist plays notes either side of the root (but not the root itself) in bar 1.4. A more extreme example occurs in bars 3.9–3.10, where the majority of pitches clash with the underlying chord of E♭ major. In bebop, dissonances of this sort are rarely resolved onto chord notes.

The first eight bars of the head reveal how the basic harmonies of *Four* are elaborately varied from the outset. The chord pattern of the first four bars is | E♭ | E♭ | E♭m⁷| A♭⁷ |. The pianist begins by adding a major 7th and a major 9th to the tonic chord (E♭△9) and then piano and bass rise through the chromatic progression Fm⁷– F#dim7 to a first inversion of E♭△9 (G in the bass) in bar H2. The four chords are very short and are 'pushed' before the beat. All of this results in the E♭ tonality of the music emerging only gradually, rather than being clearly established from the start.

When the opening four bars are repeated sequentially in bars H4–H8, the melodic sequence in the solo part is a perfect 5th lower. However, the free harmonic sequence in the accompaniment begins a major 2nd higher, (chords based on F, G, A♭ and F, rather than on E♭, F, F# and E♭) thus adding to the harmonic complexity.

The melody in bars H5–H6 outlines an E♭-major triad, ending on a blue (i.e. flat) 3rd, so might seem to bear little relation to the underlying F-minor harmony. However, E♭, G and B♭ are the 7th, 9th and 11th respectively above the root (F). This concentration on the dissonant upper extensions of chords is, as we saw *above* with the piano chord in bar H10, another characteristic of bebop.

Melody and rhythm

The theme is based on the three-note figure heard at the start and has a modest compass of a 10th, in the middle range of the trumpet. The fragmentary, scalic nature of this material is the trigger for an exploration of scalic figures over a much greater melodic range in the first two and a half choruses. Many of these involve chromatic patterns, although Davis has a preference for a gapped chromatic descent that avoids the flattened 7th (D♭), as in bars 1.1, 1.14, 1.29, 2.2–2.3 and 2.22. He makes almost no reference to the melody of the theme in these improvised choruses. Instead, Davis substitutes a series of short motifs, each of which he briefly develops before moving on to the next idea.

Blue notes, notably the flat 3rd and flat 7th (G♭ and D♭ in the key of E♭ major) are an integral part of jazz, and figure prominently at the end of the first two phrases of the head. Elsewhere, Davis plays away from the chord so often that it is difficult to distinguish blue notes from a generally chromatic approach to melody.

The predominantly quaver-based rhythm gives way to longer note values when Davis needs time to use the extended techniques mentioned earlier. Towards the end of NAM 50 longer note lengths are used again for the first significant exploration of wide leaps in bars 3.19–3.24. As the extract fades out, quavers return, but in a new pattern of repeated notes on single pitches.

The pulse is as elusive as the tonality at the start, with few of the chords on downbeats and phrases that neither start nor end on a strong beat. A clearer sense of the beat arrives with the tentative introduction of the walking bass in bar H9, although it is not until the choruses that this becomes continuous. From there on, bass and drums combine to provide a firm rhythmic backing against which Miles Davis can project his own syncopations.

Exercise 6

1. What are the main stylistic features of bebop?

2. Explain what is meant by a head arrangement.

3. What does it mean for a jazz musician to push a chord?

4. What is meant in jazz by playing away from the chord?

5. What is a ghost note?

6. What type of chord is played by the pianist on the last quaver of bar H1?

7. Which notes are blue notes in the first eight bars of the trumpet solo?

8. What do you understand is meant by a substitution chord in jazz? Give an example of a substitution chord used in *Four*.

New York Counterpoint: movement 2 (Reich)

Steve Reich first achieved fame in the late 1960s as one of several composers who rejected the complexity and dissonance of much art music of the mid 20th-century in favour of a less intellectual style in which simple musical patterns are subjected to systematic processes of gradual transformation. At first described as process music or systems music, this is the style that we now call **Minimalism**.

Although Reich's music has become more complex and multi-layered over the years, the repetition of short patterns continues to play an important part in his work. He has also retained a lively interest in music technology, writing many works that combine pre-recorded and live performance, or that use synthesisers.

Style and context

NAM 12 (page 176)	CD1 Track 16
Roger Heaton	

New York Counterpoint was commissioned by the Fromm Music Foundation (one of America's most important patrons of new music) for the clarinettist Richard Stolzman. Written in 1985, it is part of Reich's series of 'counterpoint' works that each explore the idea of a soloist playing live against a backing tape they recorded earlier.

Reich had used the idea of an instrumentalist pre-recording some elements of the performance in various earlier pieces, but this particular series started with *Vermont Counterpoint* (for flute) in 1982 and has continued with *Electric Counterpoint* (for electric guitar) written for Pat Metheny in 1987, and *Cello Counterpoint* (2003). *New York Counterpoint* can also be played entirely live (by an ensemble of 11 clarinettists) and Reich has approved an arrangement of the work for live and pre-recorded saxophones.

The first performance of *New York Counterpoint* was given by Richard Stolzman on 20 January 1986 at the Avery Fisher Hall in New York. The title of the work refers to the bustling city life reflected in the energetic, syncopated rhythms of the music and the complex contrapuntal textures that are generated by the staggered entries of the clarinet parts.

New York Counterpoint consists of three movements, in the order fast–slow–fast. NAM 12 is the central movement, although its use of mainly semiquaver patterns gives the rhythm a much greater sense of urgency than in most slow movements.

Tonality

Reich uses the key signature of B major, but since the clarinet is a transposing instrument the music will sound a tone lower than written when played on the standard clarinet in B♭. Similarly, the bass clarinet parts will sound a 9th lower – that is, an octave plus a tone. Since all the parts transpose in a similar way, we will refer only to the pitches that you see in the score, rather than to the actual sounds you hear on the recording.

The music is entirely **diatonic** – there is not a single accidental in NAM 12. Reich doesn't use functional harmony or cadences to define key, and although he uses the key signature of B major, the principal focus of the movement often centres upon the pitch E. We could therefore say that it is in the **lydian mode** on E, shown *left*. This differs from a scale of E major in having a raised fourth degree (A♯), marked ∗ in the example.

Furthermore, the melodic parts are restricted to the notes of a **hexatonic** (six-note) scale – the seventh pitch (D♯) occurs only in the pulsating **homorhythmic** textures that periodically combine with the counterpoint. The first of these starts in bar 27, but even here the tonic triad of B major reiterated in parts 7–9 is clouded by a repeated C♯ in part 10.

Structure

In older styles, composers used contrasts in key and thematic material to construct their music, as we saw in NAM 18, for example. There are no such contrasts here – in fact, the opening two-bar motif is heard in one form or another throughout the whole movement. Instead, Reich structures his music through the careful control of texture.

Although the movement is not punctuated by cadences, it falls into two distinct sections:

Bars 1–26 are characterised by a steady build-up of contrapuntal complexity with parts initially entering in pairs:

➤ Two parts in the first two bars

➤ Four parts in bars 3–8

➤ More parts are added at bar 9, but initially these double existing strands for four bars, so a real six-part texture doesn't emerge until bar 13

➤ A seventh part is added from bar 21.

In the second section (bars 27–72), clarinets 1–6 continue with various permutations of this contrapuntal texture, but the live clarinettist breaks free to take on a more soloistic role. This section is also distinguished by the addition of three dissonant four-part chords, each played as repeated semiquavers. These fade in and out on clarinets 7–10. The first two chords last for six bars and the third for eight, after which the entire pattern repeats. The homorhythmic texture thus introduced makes a vivid contrast with the counterpoint that continues around it, but finally the chords disappear, leaving six more bars of fading counterpoint, followed by a three-note fragment of the opening motif in the final bar.

> Note that the symbol 𝄎 in the score is an instruction to repeat the previous two bars, while the symbol 𝄏 is an instruction to repeat the previous bar.

Many Minimalist composers use a technique known as **phasing**, in which two repeating patterns gradually move from being in phase (when they coincide) to being out of phase (when they do not coincide). A very simple example is shown *right*.

Phasing

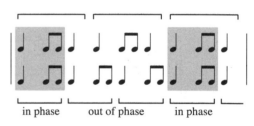

in phase   out of phase   in phase

In this work, phasing can most clearly be seen in the opening bars. For clarity the example *below* shows only the upper of each pair of parts and it omits the repeat signs. When the live clarinet enters in bar 3 it plays the same motif as clarinet 7, but half a beat later. When heard against the original motif (which continues in clarinet 7) it is a half-beat out of phase, and this creates a **canon**:

Only four notes are imitated at this point – the greyed-out notes are replaced by rests. But look at bar 5 and you will see that the canon continues despite the missing notes. Reich fills in one more note (A♯) in bar 6 – and after this the live clarinet gets to play the entire canonic entry, still half a beat out of phase.

Now look at the live clarinet entry in bar 13 of the score. Do you see that it has now moved one whole beat out of phase? The importance of the phasing process is that it causes expected rhythmic accents to be thrown 'out of sync', giving rise to complex new patterns as metrically different versions of the same idea are heard simultaneously.

Melody

The entire piece is based on the short hexatonic melody first played by clarinet 7 in bars 1–2. It is largely descending in shape and it outlines chords IV and V of B major (the triads of E major and F♯ major respectively) – see the section on harmony *below*.

This melody is paralleled, note-for-note, by clarinet 8 which plays mainly a 10th lower (that is, an octave plus a 3rd). Almost all of the imitative entries consist of similar pairings, so the counterpoint of the title occurs between different *pairs* of parts.

At bar 25 the live clarinet appears to have an independent part. This is, in fact, a **resultant melody** – a part assembled from tiny fragments of other parts sounding at the same time. Look at the live clarinet part in bar 25 and see how:

➢ the first two semiquavers come from clarinet 2

➢ the next two semiquavers are from clarinet 3

➢ the B at the start of beat 2 is from clarinet 1

➢ the B and G♯ after the first rest are from clarinet 2 … and so on.

Harmony

The repetitions of the two-bar patterns create melodic **ostinati** which centre on an hypnotic alternation of the chords of E major and F♯ major, but the phasing causes the chords to overlap and change at different times in different parts. The harmonic basis of the work can more easily be seen if we show the accompaniment to the live clarinet as follows (for clarity the parts for clarinets 1–3 are transposed down an octave):

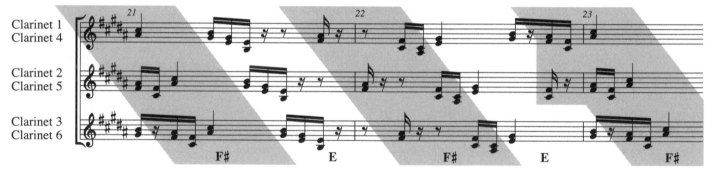

The constant overlap of these two chords generates numerous diatonic dissonances as the texture thickens, but the repetition blends them into a gentle wash of harmonic colour that never resolves to B major.

However, with the arrival of the first homorhythmic interjection comes the first use of D♯ and therefore much more gritty harmony. The three different chords heard in this section are:

➢ B major over C♯ in the bass (bars 27–32)

➢ A chord based on 4ths (E, A♯, D♯, G♯) in bars 33–38, and

➢ F♯ major over G♯ in the bass (bars 39–46).

These three pulsating chords are then repeated. They do not have a harmonic function – there is no progression towards a tonic. Their purpose is to provide contrast with the two chords of the counterpoint by adding to the dissonance level, as well as by offering a contrasting texture and different rhythm.

Instrumentation

Notable aspects of the work include its use of a single instrumental colour (clarinet tone) and the use of technology (multi-track recording) to enable all 11 parts to be delivered by a single performer. The clarinet parts cover a modest range of just over two octaves (extended to two and a half octaves for the bass clarinet). Nevertheless, this is enough to exploit the distinctively different timbres of the clarinet in low, middle and upper registers, and Reich's control over textural change ensure plenty of variety.

Exercise 7

1. How do the clarinet parts in the first two bars relate to each other?

2. How do the parts played by clarinet 5 and the live clarinettist in bars 3–6 relate to the music heard in bars 1–2?

3. In which bar does the live clarinettist start playing a resultant melody?

4. Define what is meant by phasing, giving an example from bar 21 onwards in NAM 12.

5. What is meant by saying that this movement is entirely diatonic?

6. Most of the melodic material in NAM 12 derives from the motif heard in its first two bars. How does Reich create variety in this movement?

7. To what extent do you feel that playing to a backing tape in *New York Counterpoint* compromises the spontaneity of live performance?

Sample questions

In Section C of the Unit 6 paper there will be two essay questions about a group of the instrumental works that you have studied. You must answer one of these, writing in continuous prose. The clarity of your expression, spelling and grammar will be taken into account in the marking.

Remember that it is important to give locations of each specific feature that you mention, but there should not normally be any need to write out music examples. You will be allowed to refer to an unmarked copy of NAM as you write.

Here are two essay topics to use for practice. Aim to complete each essay in 50 minutes.

(a) Comment on the ways in which ternary structures are used in the three pieces listed below:

  • Debussy, *Prélude à L'Après-midi d'un faune* (NAM 5, pages 86–119)
  • Brahms, Piano Quintet in F minor, Op. 34: movement III (NAM 18, pages 231–241)
  • Poulenc, Sonata for Horn, Trumpet and Trombone: movement I (NAM 19, pages 242–245)

(b) Compare and contrast the use of harmony and textures in the three following works:

  • Holborne, Pavane 'The image of melancholy' and Galliard 'Ecce quam bonum'
    (NAM 13, pages 191–193)
  • Haydn, String Quartet in E♭, Op. 33, No. 2 'The Joke': movement IV (NAM 16, pages 202-206)
  • *Four* (opening), as recorded by The Miles Davis Quintet (NAM 50, pages 468–470)

Applied music

Sonata pian' e forte (Giovanni Gabrieli)

Context

> NAM 14 (page 194)   CD2 Track 3
> His Majesty's Sagbutts and Cornetts
> Directed by Timothy Roberts

Venice is a small city, situated on a group of islands in a lagoon at the head of the Adriatic, but it accrued enormous wealth through its position on the trade route between Europe and the far east. As a result, Venetians were able to erect palaces and churches of the utmost splendour to line the banks of the city's canals, and to impress visitors with the scale of their entertainment and music.

Most magnificent of all was the palace of their elected leader (the Doge) and its chapel of St Mark (now a cathedral), where Giovanni Gabrieli was appointed organist in 1585. In the late Renaissance, it became famous for **polychoral** music, in which separate choirs of singers and/or instrumentalists were positioned in galleries around the building, to perform in **antiphony** – a texture in which one group dramatically answers the music of another, and all join together for spectacular climaxes – the live equivalent of 'surround sound' (a technique also used by Gabrieli in NAM 27).

> The separated choirs in polychoral music are known as **cori spezzati** in Italian ('divided choirs'). At this time the term 'choir' simply meant a group of performers, not necessarily singers.

The *Sonata pian' e forte* comes from a collection of works for eight to 15 instruments by Gabrieli, published in 1597 at the end of the Renaissance, and is famous for being among the earliest works in which any composer had indicated dynamic levels (*pian'* is an abbreviation of piano) as well as precise details of instrumentation. It is not known for what purpose the work was written, but it may have been played during a service at St Mark's, or perhaps to accompany one of the magnificent state processions into the great chapel on special festivals.

Instrumental forces

NAM 14 is written for two four-part 'choirs' of instruments (coro I and coro II in the score). Both contain three trombone parts and on CD2 each also includes a chamber organ (which can only just be heard). Gabrieli did not write parts for the organs, but by 1597 it was becoming common practice for an organ to be used to support music intended for the church.

The top part in coro I is for a cornett, a wooden wind instrument of the Renaissance, with a mouthpiece similar to that of a brass instrument, but a softer tone than the trumpet (see *left*). Do not confuse it with the cornet, which is a brass-band instrument.

The top part in coro II is labelled 'violin', but in the 16th century this could refer to several different sizes of the violin family. In this sonata the range of the part dictates that it could be played on a viola (in bar 28 it descends to D a perfect 4th lower than the modern violin's lowest note). A viola is used for this part on CD2.

The parts for trombones 1 and 2 use the tenor C clef. This indicates that the second line down on the stave is middle C. Thus the first note of the sonata is D, a tone above middle C.

Despite the fact that Gabrieli specified the instruments required, this piece is not clearly instrumental in style (as is true of most instrumental music of the late Renaissance). Each part has a narrow range and moves mainly by step, with occasional small leaps, and could easily be sung if it had words.

Most of the sonata is written in the **dorian mode**, which can be found by playing an octave of white notes on the piano from D to the D above. Gabrieli transposes this mode to G, giving the notes G–A–Bb–C–D–E–F–G. However, accidentals are used to avoid awkward intervals, to form a **tierce de Picardie** at the end of important sections (including the final plagal cadence), and to construct cadences such as the **phrygian cadence** in bars 44–45.

Tonality

The word sonata in the title of NAM 14 meant, at this time, nothing more than a piece to be played (from *sonare*, to sound) as opposed to a cantata, which was a piece to be sung (from *cantare*, to sing). It didn't imply any particular structure. In fact, this piece is **through-composed** with sections being clarified by textures and dynamics rather than by large-scale repetition of material, as shown below. Notice that most sections overlap and that the term **tutti** (all) indicates a section in which all the performers are playing:

Structure

Bars	
1–14	Opening statement (Coro I)
14–25	Answering statement (Coro II)
26–31	*Tutti* (Coro I and Coro II)
31–71	Mainly short antiphonal exchanges between Coro I and Coro II, often of similar material (e.g. bars 37–40), and each followed by a *tutti*
71–80	*Tutti*, with extensive use of **imitation**, particularly of the dotted figure first heard in the lowest part of bar 71

Although it was highly unusual at this time to specify dynamics, they follow a simple plan in clarifying the structure outlined *above*. Essentially, Gabrieli uses *piano* when just one of the choirs is playing, and *forte* when both choirs play together.

The texture is dominated by the dark sonority of the six trombones, instruments associated with solemnity and priestly ritual. The range of polychoral textures includes:

Texture and harmony

➢ The opposition of two instrumental choirs (bars 1–13 and 14–25)

➢ The combination of these same groups (bars 26–31)

➢ Short antiphonal exchanges (bars 37–40)

➢ Short homophonic sections, sometimes featuring echo effects (bars 45–49)

➢ Imitative counterpoint (e.g. the entries marked *forte* in bars 71–72).

Two other matters add to the solemnity of the music:

➢ The textures are never less than four-part (one complete choir)

➢ There is a preponderance of root-position triads, such as those in the **circle of 5ths** that occurs in bars 36–41.

By 1597, when the *Sonata pian' e forte* was first published, the modal harmony of the Renaissance was starting to give way to the tonal harmony of the early Baroque period.

It should not come as a surprise that many of the features of this piece, such as its largely contrapuntal texture and essentially modal nature (with occasional hints of modern tonality, as in the section starting at bar 45) are similar to those we noted in the study of the two dances by Holborne. NAM 13 was, in fact, first published just two years after this sonata by Gabrieli.

Finally, many of the important harmonic features of the music can be seen in the following quotation of bars 12^3–17:

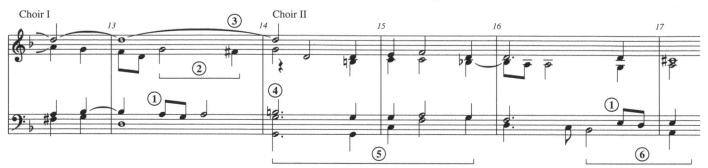

1   passing dissonances (such as these accented passing notes)
2   a suspension (and its resolution)
3   F♯ is outside the mode but it allows a perfect cadence on G
4   B♮ is a tierce de Picardie
5   a progression of modal root-position triads
6   two chords (IVb–V in D minor) that form a phrygian cadence.

Exercise 8

1.   Why is St Mark's, Venice particularly significant in the context of this work?

2.   Explain the terms *cori spezzati* and antiphonal texture.

3.   When both choirs first play together in bar 26 on what chord do they start?

4.   Which sections does Gabrieli mark *piano* and which does he mark *forte*?

5.   With what type of cadence does the sonata end? How is the final chord of this cadence modified?

6.   How does Gabrieli's use of the term choir (*coro*) differ from our use of the word today?

7.   Explain what is meant by (i) polychoral music, and (ii) a cornett.

Cantata No. 48: movements 1–4 (Bach)

Context

NAM 28 (page 288)   CD3 Tracks 3–6
Yorkshire Bach Choir
Fitzwilliam Ensemble
Clare Mathias (alto)
Conducted by Peter Seymour

A cantata is a work for one or more voices with accompaniment. NAM 48 consists of the first four (of seven) movements from a sacred cantata by J. S. Bach. Cantatas of this sort were performed during the main service on Sundays and religious festivals in the principal Lutheran churches of major cities in Protestant Germany during the late Baroque period.

In 1723 Bach was appointed to direct the music at St Thomas in Leipzig, a position that he held until his death in 1750. His duties included providing weekly cantatas for performance by the choir and small orchestra, most of whose members came from the boys' school where Bach taught and that was attached to the church.

The texts of Bach's cantatas were related to the bible readings for the day concerned and consisted of German verse, biblical quotations and one or more hymns (known in Germany as chorales). In his early years in Leipzig, it is believed that Bach wrote at least 300 church cantatas. Only one was published in his lifetime and, while some 200 have survived in manuscripts, it is thought that at least 100 were lost after the composer's death.

Bach's cantatas include a huge variety of music, from works for solo voice with orchestra (probably sung by one of Bach's many unfortunate sons when the rest of the choir was on holiday) to large-scale cantatas for festive occasions that would have required extra musicians from the city and its university. The cantatas also encompass almost every type of music known to Bach, from the most serious counterpoint to the jolliest of dance styles.

Scholars have been able to establish that the first performance of Cantata 48 was almost certainly given on Sunday 3 October 1723, so it dates from Bach's first few months in Leipzig. It follows the pattern of most of his cantatas by including:

➤ Elaborate pieces for choir and orchestra (movement 1)

➤ Harmonised chorale tunes with melodies that the congregation would have known and might possibly have joined in singing (movement 3)

➤ Music based on types of music commonly used in opera at this time, such as **recitative** (movement 2) and **aria** (movement 4).

The musicians available to Bach at St Thomas included a small all-male choir of up to 16 members (with boys singing the soprano and alto parts, and men singing the tenor and bass parts), and a string ensemble of about ten players (1st violins, 2nd violins, violas, cellos and a violone – a precursor of the double bass).

To these were added any additional instruments that Bach required for the work concerned. In this cantata they were:

➤ Two oboes (the second of which simply plays in a few of the movements, where it doubles the first oboe)

➤ A part labelled 'tromba', which means trumpet – however, the trumpets of Bach's day had no valves and therefore could not easily have played all of the notes required in this cantata, so it is possible that the part might have been played on trumpet with a trombone-like slide or on a cornett (see page 62).

In addition, the harmony would always have been filled out by an organist, using the figures and symbols printed under the bass part as a guide to the chords required. For example, '7' in bar 1 indicates a 7th above the bass note C, which in this context indicates a chord of Cm^7).

This type of part is known as a **figured bass**, and the instruments that play the part (cello, violone and organ, in this case) are known as **continuo** instruments. The harmonic infilling provided by the continuo (which might also include the harpsichord and lute) is one of the most characteristic sounds of Baroque music, and helps to distinguish it from the musical styles of other periods.

A translation of the German text is given on page 538 of NAM.

The three final movements, not in NAM, are a recitative and an aria for tenor soloist and then the chorale on which the first movement is based.

Performing forces

The performance on CD3 uses a large mixed choir and modern instruments (including a trumpet). For different interpretations of the work, try searching on *YouTube* for performances of Cantata 48 directed by Harnoncourt or Gardiner.

Movement 1
Chorus

1st movement

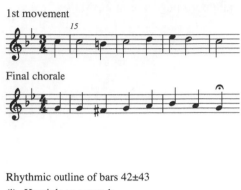

Rhythmic outline of bars 42±43

(i) Hemiola as notated:

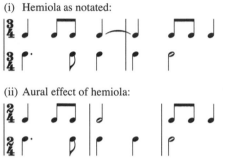

(ii) Aural effect of hemiola:

Movement 2
Recitative

Word setting is described as syllabic when there is generally just one note for each syllable of text. When many notes are set to a single syllable, as at the end of the first movement, the word setting is described as melismatic.

Listen to the first movement and then state where the opening 12 bars are repeated exactly. Did you notice that these bars also appear in abbreviated versions in other places? This is known as **ritornello form**. Ritornello means 'a little return' and reflects the use of shortened repetitions (between contrasting **episodes**) as a structural device. The ritornello here is characterised by minor keys, sequences and discords (on the first beats of bars 1, 2, 6 and 8) that underline the rather grim text.

An adaptation of the chorale melody with which the complete cantata ends is played in **canon** by the trumpet and oboes (see *left*). A pre-existing melody (such as this) against which other tunes are set in counterpoint is known as a **cantus firmus**. Around the cantus firmus the choir declaims the text in a succession of imitative entries (often canonic in style, but not strictly in canon), and below both sets of parts the ritornello emerges frequently in the type of contrapuntal complexity for which Bach is famous.

The music is mainly in G minor with modulations to related minor keys (again reflecting the solemn text). Most of the main sections end with a rhythmic device called a **hemiola**. This has the effect of highlighting the cadences by making two bars of $\frac{3}{4}$ time sound like three bars of $\frac{2}{4}$ (see *left*) and is found in much triple-time Baroque music. Notice the calming effect of the long tonic pedal at the end of this movement, and the **tierce de Picardie** in the final cadence.

Listen to the word-setting in this movement. Do you notice that it is entirely different from the first movement? The text flows past at a much faster rate, the word setting is almost entirely **syllabic**, the rhythms seem to reflect those of natural speech and the accompaniment is purely supportive. This is called **recitative**. Notice how Bach modulates rapidly through a number of keys and uses dissonant and chromatic chords to express the text.

Recitative is often accompanied by continuo instruments alone, as in the opening of NAM 36. When parts for other instruments are included, such as the sustained parts for strings used here, the music is described as accompanied recitative (despite the fact that recitative supported only by continuo instruments is not literally unaccompanied!).

The somewhat lurid text is of a type very popular among some German Protestants at the time and is expressed through:

➤ Detached melodic fragments to highlight the sighs and dramatic expressions of self-contempt ('O the pain, O the misery')

➤ Angular melodic lines with tortured leaps such as the diminished 7th on *Elend!* (misery) in bar 2

➤ Extreme dissonance such as the minor 9th between the singer and the bass on the first beat of bar 2

➤ Modulation to a foreign key at bar 10, where the music suddenly moves to E major at the words *stärkste Gift* (strongest poison).

Listen to the recording and try to spot how the singer embellishes the repeated quavers at the start of bars 7, 11 and 14. Such decoration is typical of the performing practices of Bach's day.

This chorale tune was already at least 100 years old when Bach included it in Cantata 48. The melody is purely **diatonic**, but it is totally transformed by Bach's **chromatic** harmonisation. The use of chords such as the diminished 7th allows some unexpected modulations to G minor (bar 2) and A♭ major (bar 6). Instead of the expected perfect cadence in B♭ major at the end of the melody, Bach introduces an A♭ which sparks off a series of anguished suspensions (for instance, the alto G♭ against the tenor F in bar 9).

If you are working on chorales for the technical study in Unit 5, this is a valuable opportunity to hear one performed – notice that it is played by instruments as well as sung by four-part choir, and that the double bass sounds an octave below the printed bass. However, the chromatic style adopted by Bach to portray the text of this particular chorale is considerably more complex than the style of harmonisation expected in exam submissions.

Movement 3
Chorale

The fourth movement is an obbligato aria – a song with an equally important (obligatory) instrumental solo. When you listen to it try to note where and how the opening music returns. Did you spot that sometimes only little fragments of it come back? For instance, the singer starts with the opening four bars of oboe music, and in bars 23–24 the oboe itself plays a fragment from bars 5–6. Do you recognise this musical form?

Movement 4
Aria

Supporting the duet between singer and oboe is a bass that moves almost entirely in quavers. This is a much earlier example of the type of 'walking bass' that we saw in Miles Davis' *Four*.

The aria is in E♭ major and falls into two main sections. The first ends in the dominant key of B♭ major at bar 38 while the second moves straight into C minor and then passes through a number of closely related keys before returning to E♭ major in the perfect cadence of bars 78–79. The performance direction *D.C. al Fine* – repeat from the beginning as far as the word *Fine* (finish) – means that the opening ritornello (bars 1–16) should then be repeated to conclude the aria.

Exercise 9

1. Which of the four movements in NAM 28 have a homophonic texture and which are contrapuntal?

2. What is a cantus firmus? How is the cantus firmus treated in the first movement of NAM 28?

3. Name three similarities between the final cadence of Bach's first movement and the final cadence of Gabrieli's *Sonata pian' e forte* on page 199 of NAM.

4. What type of keyboard instrument would you expect to play a continuo part in a church cantata?

5. Explain the difference between melismatic and syllabic word setting, giving examples of each.

6. What are the main differences between the recitative and aria?

7. Name the obbligato instrument used in the aria.

8. What is a chorale? Describe two different ways in which Bach uses a chorale in NAM 28.

9. For what type of musical texture is Bach famous?

On the Waterfront: Symphonic Suite (Bernstein)

Context

NAM 43 (page 374)   CD4 Track 2
New York Philharmonic
Conducted by Leonard Bernstein

Bernstein's most famous musical, *West Side Story*, was completed in 1957 and reflects the musical style of *On the Waterfront* in some of its numbers.

The 1954 film *On the Waterfront* tells a story, based on reality, of crime and extortion in New York's dockland, and of the struggle of a young dock worker (played by Marlon Brando) who fought against the corrupt practices exposed in the film. It was in stark contrast to the romantic comedies and Hollywood epics usually seen in the cinema and its harsh social realism made a great impact.

Leonard Bernstein had achieved success in writing musicals for the theatre before being asked to compose the music for this film. Some of these musicals had been filmed, but *On the Waterfront* was the only actual film score that he ever wrote. The social realism of the film does not entirely extend to its music, which is scored for the typically large symphony orchestra of big-budget American movies. However the exhilarating percussion rhythms and fearsome brass writing (both characteristic of Bernstein's style) give the music a hard edge which echoes the intensity and violence of the film. In 1955 Bernstein arranged some of the music from the film into a symphonic suite for performance in concert halls, and it is from the opening of this version that NAM 43 is taken.

Instrumentation

When reading the score note that:

Tip: When a pitch is included in the name of a transposing instrument it tells you the note that will sound when C is played. For example, a horn in F will sound F when C is played.

➤ The clarinet in E♭ sounds a minor 3rd higher than written while the alto saxophone in E♭ sounds a major 6th lower than written

➤ Clarinets and trumpets in B♭ sound a tone lower, and the bass clarinet in B♭ sounds a major 9th lower, than written

➤ Horns in F sound a perfect 5th lower than written

➤ The piccolo sounds an octave higher, while the double bassoon and double basses sound an octave lower, than written.

Bernstein's orchestration is dominated by wind and percussion, while strings have little independent material before bar 88 and mainly double other parts – Bernstein treats the orchestra like a huge jazz band. Only in the last four pages of the extract are the strings given a role of their own, and even then it is more in the nature of a special effect, sustaining single pitches or icy dissonances against the forceful interjections of wind and percussion.

Slow introduction

The very high notes in the horn and trumpet solos are technically very demanding, especially since there is little or no accompaniment and the dynamics are mainly quiet. Notice that Bernstein cues them into other parts (shown by small notes) in case alternatives are needed.

The work opens with a long **monophonic** melody for solo horn. Its notes are taken from a blues scale on F (sounding pitches) whose **blue notes** (the flattened 3rd, 5th and 7th, marked * *left*) help to establish a desolate, mournful mood at this slow speed.

Starting in bar 7, the opening theme is repeated in two-part **canon** between the unusual combination of flutes (in octaves) and muted trombone. The blues is again evident at the start of bar 11, where the flat 5th (C♭) in the flutes clashes against B♭ in the trombone.

The second part of this theme then appears on muted trumpet (bar 13), a 4th higher than in bar 4 and sounding *lontano* (distant). The simple two-part harmonisation is underpinned by a pedal on F, sustained by clarinets and articulated by the harp.

When the clarinets move off this pedal at the end of bar 17 they play fragments of the first part of the theme in 'subtone' (very quiet and breathy) – Bernstein has returned to the monophonic texture of the opening, but now heard in bare octaves. Finally, in bar 19 the ascending minor 3rd of this motif is transformed into a major 3rd in preparation for the next section.

The sparse scoring of this introduction for wind and harp reflects the film's theme of a lonely individual faced with a regime of corrupt practices. It contrasts strongly with the percussive *Presto* that follows, with its depiction of the seething, dangerous atmosphere of the New York docks in the 1950s.

Presto barbaro means fast and barbaric, and its two time signatures indicate that bars of ₵ and ¾ alternate. It begins with a six-bar syncopated idea for piano and timpani (played with hard sticks) that features the rising minor 3rds from the opening theme of the work, joined by its major-3rd variant in bar 24.

Presto barbaro

'Una corda' in bar 20 of the piano part is an instruction to use the left-hand ('soft') pedal.

A second timpanist enters in bar 26, playing the rhythm of bars 20–21 on C♯ and F♯, forming dissonances of a **tritone** and a major 7th respectively above the continuing pedal on G. In bar 32 three drums of different pitch levels join in with an outline of the same idea. The effect is like the start of a very dissonant fugue for percussion.

The three percussion parts come together in bar 40 to form a **riff** which then accompanies a loud jazz-like solo for alto saxophone. Bernstein marks this 'crudely', leaving little doubt about the brash atmosphere he wishes to create. The sax melody consists of three four-bar phrases, the first two of which are similar. This is the melodic structure of a 12-bar blues, but there is no sign of a blues-based chord pattern. The sax and lowest timpani notes focus on notes from a blues scale on G, but the high level of dissonance leaves the music sounding essentially atonal.

In bar 53 the side drummer plays a rim shot (explained in the margin note on page 54). This type of accented off-beat ending is another Bernstein fingerprint.

In bar 54 high wind instruments enter with a compressed version of the sax melody in which the long notes have been shortened. This melody is a 3rd higher than before, although the timpani riff (now joined by lower strings) remains on the original pitches.

The dynamic level drops dramatically and the texture thins in bars 62–63, but the drum rhythm continues and almost immediately Bernstein begins another build-up as he develops the cadential saxophone motif from bar 52. Starting in bar 64, this is played by first violins and oboes, combined with its own inversion in the second-violin and clarinet parts. Two bars later, low strings and bassoons add variants of the falling 4th idea from bar 44.

Tremolo upper strings and timpani rolls add to a cresendo which culminates in a powerful tutti at bar 78, where the whole orchestra stamps out the percussion patterns in dissonant block chords. Notice how Bernstein increases the impact of this section by adding further dissonances above the already discordant riff. The texture is not just homophonic but **homorhythmic** (all parts having exactly the same rhythm for ten bars).

The rhythm of the percussion riff is maintained by a solitary side drum from bar 88, while high sustained strings (punctuated by upper woodwind) remind us of figures from the sax solo that started in bar 42. Rising and falling semitones converge on a unison in the violins, the latter replaced by the falling 4th in bar 94. The pattern is reversed in bar 98: a unison D♭ expands outwards to form a major 2nd on C and D♮, sustained by high woodwind, trumpets and violins, below which the timpani return. To support the increasing dynamic, more instruments are added, the violins re-energise their major second with tremolo, the E♭ clarinet trills between C and D (notated as a tremolo), the flutes, piccolo, oboes and trumpets use flutter-tonguing (*flutt.* in bar 105, produced by rolling an 'r' with the tongue while blowing), a roll on a suspended cymbal brings the crescendo to its climax and at last the rhythmic ostinato (heard constantly since bar 20) ceases on the pause chord in bar 105.

In bar 105, the phrase ***dura come*** $\frac{3}{2}$ means that the pause should last the length of three minim beats.

Coda (Adagio)

Starting in bar 106, the eight-bar **coda** begins with a slow and very loud restatement of the motif from bar 52. Beneath it Bernstein reaffirms the importance of the tritone in this music by slowly superimposing two triads a tritone apart (F major and B major – the 3rd of the latter enharmonically notated as E♭ rather than D♯).

This colossal dissonance is hammered out by wind and percussion in bars 108–109. In the rests, the strings can be heard very quietly sustaining the same dissonance using the thin, icy tone produced by playing *sul ponticello* (with the bow close to the bridge).

In the last four bars Bernstein uses a similar pattern but ratchets up the dissonance still further. This time a triad of E major (the 3rd again enharmonically notated as A♭) is overlaid by the note B♭ (a tritone above E) plus a further tritone formed by C and F♯.

Because the bass in the coda moves down a semitone from F to E while the upper part moves up from A to B, there is sense that the music has reached a stopping point. But this is no cadence – the atonality of these bars is even more forceful than the dissonances of bebop jazz that had so influenced Bernstein in the early 1950s.

Leonard Bernstein described the work from which NAM 43 is taken as a 'symphonic suite'. He wrote it for a symphony orchestra, but he used its resources more like a huge jazz band. Perhaps what he really meant by 'symphonic' is the way in which he develops and exploits his motifs with much greater rigour than can be found in most earlier film scores.

Exercise 10

1. In which bars does Bernstein use each of the following textures? (i) homophonic, (ii) monophonic, (iii) two-part counterpoint.

2. What are the sounding pitches of the first two horn notes in bar 1?

3. Explain the meaning of 'con sord.' (trombone, bar 7) and 'subtone' (clarinets, bar 17).

4. What two features do bars 20 and 78 have in common?

5. Explain how the trumpet and alto saxophone parts are related in bars 52–53.

6. Describe the two different types of tremolo on page 385 of NAM.

7. The film *On the Waterfront* sometimes depicts an atmosphere of bleak despair, but at other times a mood of anger. Show how Bernstein's music reflects both of these moods.

Planet of the Apes: The Hunt (opening) (Goldsmith)

The American composer Jerry Goldsmith (1929–2004) studied film music before working in radio and television. He wrote the music for a popular 1960s' television series called *Dr Kildare*, but he is chiefly remembered for some 200 film scores, including *Alien* and *Star Trek: The Motion Picture* (both 1979).

Planet of the Apes (1968) centres on a group of American astronauts who become stranded on a remote planet. When they eventually stumble on life-supporting vegetation they also come face to face with a population of gorillas on horseback who, in this spectacular chase scene, succeed in capturing the humans.

The harsh images and alien landscapes of the film are reflected in the modernist style of Goldsmith's music, some parts of which are very sparse. He reserves the full forces of his large orchestra for only the most dramatic scenes, of which 'The Hunt' is one of the most memorable. NAM 44 consists of just the first part of the complete cue, which in total consists of more than five minutes' worth of continuous music in the film.

The score is written for a large symphony orchestra, to which is added a number of unusual instruments. The electric harp and electric bass clarinet that Goldsmith specified are normal acoustic instruments equipped with pick-ups. These allow the low notes of the harp to be processed with reverberation and a special 'buzz' effect, and the squeaks from the bass clarinet reed to be amplified, simulating the excited chatter of the apes at bar 52. They are joined in this bar by the ram's horn (a Jewish religious instrument called a *shofar*) and the fearsome sound of the ten-foot long Tibetan horn. Both are used to give musical expression to the frightening image of horse-riding gorillas in pursuit of humans.

Percussion instruments play an important role in developing and sustaining the drama of the chase, starting with the solo timpani notes on each downbeat of bars 1–8 and culminating in the climax at bar 52, where four percussionists are required.

As well as standard percussion (timpani, side drum, bass drum and xylophone) Goldsmith uses boo bams, timbales and friction drums (see *right*), plus a bass resin drum (a large drum with a shell made from a resin compound), a conga drum and a vibra-slap (a device that produces a chattering sound, like a rattlesnake). Notably absent are metallic percussion instruments such as the cymbals, triangle or glockenspiel, the composer preferring his wide range of drum colours plus the dry wooden sound of the xylophone to portray the fearful chase.

Although not a standard orchestral instrument, a piano introduces the main motif of the cue in octaves in bar 4, but when this is later developed into ostinato patterns (bars 11–22, 45–51 and 59–73) the piano is used mainly to articulate driving semiquaver rhythms. This percussive treatment of the piano is most evident in bars 84–91, where its syncopated and doubled major 7ths cut through a variety of other simultaneous riffs.

Context

NAM 44 (page 388)   CD4 Track 3
Conducted by Jerry Goldsmith

Planet of the Apes was remade in 2001 with a different cast, and a rather more conventional and, some have felt, less memorable score by Danny Elfman.

In film music, a cue is a more or less continuous passage of music designed for a particular point in the film.

Instrumentation

The boo bam, or tamboo bamboo, comes from Trinidad. Tamboo is a corruption of *tambour* (French for a small drum). The instrument consists of a hollowed-out and tuned bamboo stem, sounding like a small tuned bongo drum. Timbales are cylindrical drums with metal shells that produce a powerful sound with very clear attack. Notes on a friction drum are produced by vibrating the skin with a dampened cloth or fingers, or by means of a cord that passes through the drum skin.

Throughout the score Goldsmith is very specific in the effects he requires – for example, *wooden* horn mutes in bar 10, *felt* mallets for the conga drum in bar 16 and **harmonics** for the violins in bars 68–73. Starting at bar 55, the trumpets are required to use plunger mutes – rubber suction cups that result in a very thin tone when held directly in front of the bell of a brass instrument. At the same time, second and third trombones have to combine this effect with flutter-tonguing (an effect used by Bernstein in NAM 43).

Instruments are sometimes used at the extremes of their range, particularly to add to the tension of bars 55–58, where bassoon, double bassoon, first trombone, cellos and double basses are all very low, horns swoop to the top of their range, and violins, flutes and piccolo rush upwards to their own highest registers.

The orchestra on CD4 is not identified. Film soundtracks are often recorded by 'session musicians', who may include members of well-known orchestras as well as other professional musicians, who come together specifically to record the soundtrack.

Another important aspect of Goldsmith's vivid orchestration is his tendency to score much of the more prominent material for wind or piano. He uses the strings for chordal accompaniments (as in bars 1–7), short links (bar 10), special effects (such as the inverted pedals above the riff in bars 11–21) and punctuating rhythmic patterns (bars 26, 30–31 and 42–44).

When reading the score, note that:

➤ Parts marked E.H. are for English horn (cor anglais) and sound a perfect 5th lower than written

➤ Clarinets in B♭ and Trumpets in B♭ sound a tone lower than written; the bass clarinet sounds an octave plus a tone (a major 9th) lower than written

➤ Horns in F sound a perfect 5th lower than written

➤ Double basses and double bassoons sound an octave lower than written; piccolos sound an octave higher than written.

Listening guide

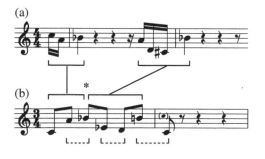

(a)

(b)

Structure in film music is usually dictated by the events on screen. This can lead to a treatment that may seem 'bitty' and unconnected, but Goldsmith guards against this by manipulating and developing short **motifs** that permeate and unify the entire film score. Most notable is the piano figure in bar 4, transposed to the treble clef in example (b), *left*. It derives from the start of the twitchy main theme of the film, shown in (a), which is heard before the extract in NAM begins. The transformation is achieved through:

➤ Changes of metre and rhythm, so that two separate ideas in (a) become the continuous quaver motif in (b)

➤ Melodically inverting the first interval of (a) – a falling minor 3rd – so that it becomes a rising major 6th in (b)

➤ Transposing the second idea in (a) by a semitone to start on B♭

➤ Linking both halves of (a) by overlapping them, so that the B♭ marked ✳ becomes both the end of the first idea and the start of the (transposed) second idea.

This transformation results in six different pitches of the 12-note chromatic scale being used in bar 4. Goldsmith repeats this motif in bar 8, but this time extends it to all 12 pitches of the chromatic scale, ending at the F♮ in bar 9. Just as (b) finished by returning to its starting note (C) in bar 5, so this extended version returns to its starting note by a further small extension (Db–C). This final semitone is not padding – it reflects the semitones heard or suggested at the start of the motif, shown by dashed brackets in (b) *opposite*, and it also looks back to the **parallel-** and **contrary-motion** semitones heard in the wind and string parts of bars 1–7. The prominent use of semitones will prove to be another a unifying idea in NAM 44.

The 12 different pitches in bars 9–10 may remind you of a note row in **serial music**. They form the chords in bars 1–3 and 5–7 (see *right*) – a serial technique known as verticalisation. Fragments from the row are manipulated to form the woodwind motifs in bars 13–22, and material derived from the row appears in many other places. However, Goldsmith doesn't use such processes in the systematic way found in most serial music – he is selective in their application. In fact, while NAM 44 is chromatic and dissonant, it is *not* **atonal**. We can see this in the way that the note C is heard as an anchor at the start of each of the first eight bars. The piano motifs in bars 4–5 and 8–10 begin on (and return to) C and are transposed to start on G (left hand) from bar 11 onwards – much more like the tonic and dominant of tonal music than the atonality of most serial music.

Goldmith uses a bar of $\frac{5}{4}$ time (bar 10) to mark the end of the first section. The piano motif from bar 4 is then transposed to start on G and turned into a bass riff, above which the right hand's offbeat semiquavers increase the rhythmic drive. These form a double pedal on G and E. If you have any doubt that 'The Hunt' is tonal at heart, despite its dissonance, notice that it is now the note G that is heard as an anchor on every down-beat in bars 11–22.

Above the riff, a high sustained violin note crescendos into an offbeat semitone at the end of bar 13. This transformation of the semitone motif from a melodic to a harmonic idea is anticipated by lower strings and harp on the second beat of bar 13 (F–E). The violin crescendo is heard three times at different pitches, but the F–E anticipation remains constant each time. Now look at the tiny figure played by flutes, piccolo and xylophone in bars 13–14. Can you see how this is related? If not, look back at (a) *opposite*. Before we move on, take note of the conga part that enters in bar 16. This increases the rhythmic tension by introducing **cross-rhythms** of two main notes per bar (effectively ♩. ♩.) against the predominant three-beat pulse (♩ ♩ ♩) of triple time.

At bar 22, a bar of $\frac{5}{4}$ time again marks the end of the section. In the next bar the tonal centre moves to Eb (there is no process of modulation), the riff transfers to electric harp and woodwind, and the trombones take over the crescendo on a sustained note (now lengthened by one beat) that was previously played by the violins.

Although Goldsmith doesn't employ such tonal devices as modulation or cadences, the use of 3rd-related tonal centres (here C, G and Eb) is not a particularly modern aspect of NAM 44. Such 'tertiary relationships' were common in 19th-century music.

Goldsmith makes further use of serial techniques by referring to the pitches of bars 8–9 (shown in the example *above*) in **retrograde** and **retrograde inversion** forms in the bass of bars 23–29. However, it is important to remember that he uses these techniques very freely (sometimes even omitting notes from the set of 12) and not in the systematic way used by serial composers.

Overview of the structure

Bars

Bars	
1–10	Introduction leading to main motif at bar 8 (centred on C)
11–22	Motif used as a riff for piano (centred on G)
23–37	Riff moves to woodwind (centred on E♭)
38–44	Build-up to the first climax at bar 42
45–51	Tonal centre returns to C
52–58	Build-up to the second climax at bar 55
59–73	Riff returns (centred on G)
74–83	Dissonant two-part counterpoint for strings
84–91	3 riffs combined as the music heads towards another climax

Notice how Goldsmith winds up the tension by adding a diminished 5th to the concluding semitone in bar 26 (G♭ in trombone 1 against C in trombone 3, while the second trombone's D♭ simultaneously supplies the semitone against C). Meanwhile, the strings play fragments of the wind parts from the start of the movement (bars 26, 30–31 and 35–37). You might also spot that the conga's cross-rhythm appears sporadically in double bass and side drum parts.

In bar 40 the idea of a long note leading to a semitonal dissonance is turned on its head – the opening note is reduced to a quaver and the offbeat semitone becomes the part of the motif that is sustained – with powerfully dissonant results. This idea forms the impetus for the repeated semitonal dissonances in the next four bars. Notice the melodic use of falling semitones in the trumpet figures and the strident cross-rhythms between strings and wind. After this first climactic section (marked out again by changes in metre) the tonal centre returns to C at bar 45. The piano riff returns, transposed to provide its articulated pedal on C, and the crescendo motif returns in abbreviated form in the horns, also on C.

This brief respite leads to a second climax at bar 52, in which the array of ethnic and electric instruments enters as the full horror of the apes on horseback becomes clear. At the bottom of the texture the lowest instruments repeatedly rise from E♭ to E♮ against a sustained E♭, creating the most earth-shaking semitonal dissonance of all. In bar 54 four horns in unison join the bellowing ram's horn, swooping to their highest register (the diagonal line indicating an upward **glissando**). And then in bar 55 Goldsmith unleashes his full orchestral resources. Adding to the elements already noted, trumpets repeatedly climb to a piercingly high dissonance (it is a semitone, of course) on which they open their plunger mutes, the third trombone growls its flutter-tongued melodic semitones, and the upper woodwind and strings pile on scales and cross-rhythms, increasing the cacophony by decorating their repeated Gs with semitones above and below.

After this brilliantly scored climax the piano riff returns (bar 59) in almost its original version, based on G. However, there are some significant changes. Bars 11–21 were in triple metre, while now we are in quadruple metre. This results in two more quavers being added to the riff (G♯ and D♯ at the end of each bar). Why these two pitches? Because they both create semitonal dissonances against the G♮–E ostinato in the pianist's right hand.

There are also changes in scoring. The violas double the pianist's right-hand ostinato, but in a rhythm of their own, and the cellos and basses also have a three-note ostinato figure. Can you see how it relates to the first three-note motif in the film's main theme, shown again in example (a), *left*?

In bars 63–64 Goldsmith transfers the crescendo on a sustained note to muted trumpets, but instead of terminating in a semitonal scrunch, it ends with a transposition of the three-note figure we noticed in bars 13–14 (shown as example (c)). Notice that this is doubled by the highly unusual combination of three piccolos in unison, as well as xylophone. This three-note figure was originally derived from the start of example (a), and in example (d) we can see

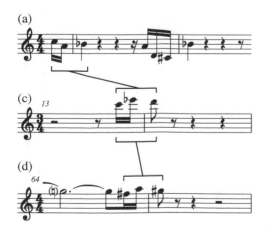

(a)

(c) *13*

(d) *64*

that it has morphed into yet another variant of the semitonal idea that has dominated this work – F♯ below the long G♮, ending with G♯ above it. Even when this in turn starts changing (bars 68–69) the omnipresent semitone is heard high above in violin harmonics (which sound two octaves above the printed black notes).

A very condensed version of the long-note-plus-semitone appears in the horn parts at bar 75, but now the urgent rhythms cease and for the first time Goldsmith uses predominately minim movement and mainly strings. They double the horns in bar 75, but sustain the terminating minor 2nd (the semitone between G and A♭). The following passage of two-part counterpoint for strings provides a brief relaxation in tension (although no respite from dissonance), designed to throw into relief the final section of the extract, which starts at bar 84. It is based on three simultaneous riffs:

➢ A much more rhythmic variant of the semitone pattern, heard high in the flutes and piccolo.

➢ Repeated clashes of a minor 2nd and its inversion (a major 7th) between the B♭s and As heard high in the piano and violin parts. First violins play on the beat, against which second violins and piano have a syncopated cross-rhythm. The latter looks more complicated than it sounds – the pattern is shown without barring by the upper notes *right*. It is the rhythm first introduced on the conga drum in bar 16, but now in $\frac{4}{4}$ instead of $\frac{3}{4}$ time.

➢ A repeated quaver-based figure in the lower strings that begins and ends with falling semitones from B♭ to A.

From the end of bar 88, the string parts in this third riff are shadowed by bassoons in crotchets, and the violas start moving in contrary motion (shadowed in crotchets by the English horn).

The repetitive rhythms of the riffs, the expansion of the third riff by contrary motion, the addition of more instruments and the accompanying side-drum rolls all increase the tension as the music moves towards the next section, signalled by a change of time signature in bar 91. There the score in NAM 44 comes to an end, but 'The Hunt' continues.

Exercise 11

1. What is the relationship between the parts for bass clarinet, first bassoon and horns in the first three notes of bar 10? Remember to take account of the transposing instruments.

2. What is the sounding pitch of the trumpet note in bar 63?

3. What term describes the relationship between all of the string and horn notes in bar 75 beat 1?

4. Compare the piano part in bars 11 and 59.

5. Explain the terms riff and cross-rhythm, giving examples of each from NAM 44.

6. What helps establish a sense of tonality in bars 1–22 of this work, and what helps to destabilise that sense of tonality?

Baris Melampahan (traditional Balinese)

Context

> NAM 59 (page 522)   CD4 Track 17
> Gong Kebyar de Sebatu

NAM 59 is an extract of traditional music from Bali, one of the thousands of islands that form the republic of Indonesia. Although Bali is smaller than the county of Devon, it has become famous as a popular tourist destination because of its tropical climate, coral reefs and rich cultural heritage in the visual and performing arts.

Baris is a traditional war dance performed by the young men of Bali to demonstrate their military skill. In its most ceremonial form it involves dressing in costumes that imitate armour, wearing distinctive pointed hats and other adornments, and carrying weapons such as lances or shields. The movements of the dance emphasise firmness of step and skill in handling weapons.

In *Baris Melampahan*, which developed in the early 20th century, the participants use the baris style to enact a dramatic scene from an ancient epic poem. This usually leads to the start of a stylised battle with which the dance ends. NAM 59 is only a short excerpt (the complete piece lasts more than 12 minutes) although it is long enough to convey the warlike quality of the dance.

> Videos of gamelan performances in *gong kebyar* style include:
> http://youtu.be/DtqGQBp0JlU
> http://youtu.be/ldPMifPbngc
>
> See also the pictures and sound files at http://web.hku.hk/~gamelano/

NAM 59 is an example of the *gamelan gong kebyar* style of performance. This, too, developed in the early 20th century and its sudden outbursts, vivid contrasts and brilliant sounds perfectly match the stylised aggression of *Baris Melampahan*. On CD4 it is played by a *gong kebyar* ensemble from Sebatu, a village in the centre of Bali, famed for maintaining important local traditions in craftwork and music.

Gamelan

NAM 59 is played on a gamelan – an ensemble of instruments consisting mainly of tuned gongs and metallophones. They are made, tuned and kept together as a set, and are not separately owned by each musician as happens in most western ensembles. Gamelan players don't regard themselves as individuals when performing, but as musicians playing one common instrument.

> Although Gamelan music on Bali is now performed mainly for tourists, the examiners will expect you to know that its origins date back thousands of years as music intended primarily to accompany rituals and ceremonies.

Every gamelan is tuned in a slightly different way, using pitches that are not directly related to western scales. NAM 59 is **pentatonic**, using five notes (1, 2, 3, 5 and 6) from the seven-note pelog scale. This set of pitches is known as the *pelog selisir* mode, and is particularly associated with the instruments used in *gong kebyar*. The five pitches are shown at the head of the score but they can only be approximated in western notation – notes 1 and 5 are a little flatter than indicated, and the others are slightly sharper by varying amounts.

In addition, a tradition in *gong kebyar* is to tune each pair of metallophones slightly differently, causing a beating effect called *ombak* when they play the same note. *Ombak* can clearly be heard in NAM 59, and helps give the music its shimmering quality.

> We say that gamelan is an oral tradition which means that its details are passed on by word of mouth (although the term 'aural tradition' might be better, as learning gamelan also involves detailed listening).

The performers memorise gamelan music and don't play from scores, but the system of notation used in NAM 59 was developed around 1900 for study purposes. However, it is quite difficult to follow as the music is very fast. You may find it easier to follow the outline described as 'Sequence' near the top of page 522 in NAM while listening to the piece.

Instruments

The various instruments in the gamelan are explained in the score. You do not need to memorise their names, as you will have an unmarked copy of NAM in the exam. However, it can be helpful to think of the instruments in four groups, each with its own function that stays the same throughout the music:

➢ *Balungan* instruments play the main melody (described *below*); they include one-octave metallophones and the *suling* (a quiet bamboo flute)

➢ *Colotomic* instruments are mainly gongs of various sizes that mark out the patterns of beats (again, see *below*)

➢ *Panususan* instruments (larger metallophones with bamboo resonators) decorate and embellish the main melody

➢ Drums and cymbals provide contrast, particularly in the loud *angsel* sections.

Rhythm

Rhythmic precision is essential in gamelan playing. Apart from the start and the ending, there is a strict pulse and a **colotomic** structure. This means a repeating pattern of beats made up of nested shorter patterns (with gongs marking the end of each one-, two- and eight-beat pattern). Before we see how this works, it is important to understand that in gamelan music the most important beat in any group is the last – not the first, as in western music. This is sometimes known as an end accent.

Now look at the first main 'B' section, which occupies the bottom system on page 523. It consists of an eight-beat rhythmic cycle called a *gongan*:

➢ The end of the eight-beat *gongan* is announced by a single stroke on the largest gong (shown by the symbol ⑥ on the *jegogan* stave)

➢ The end of the first half of the *gongan* is marked by a stroke on the *jegogan* itself – this signals the end of a four-beat pattern known as a *keteg*

➢ The *calung* plays notes that are two beats long (the second, fourth, sixth and eighth pitches of the melody described below)

➢ The *kempli* (a small time-keeping gong) plays one-beat notes (the part printed on the uppermost stave)

➢ The smallest instruments, on the lowest staves, play notes that are each only half or a quarter of a beat in length.

Melody

The basis of NAM 59 is a 'core melody' or 'nuclear melody', known as the *pokok* in Bali, the pitches of which are shown *right*. This melody is played by the *ugal* (the leading metallophone).

The dots below pitches 5 and 6 indicate that these notes are in the octave below pitches 1, 2 and 3.

Other melodic instruments form a layered texture around this part. As we have seen, the *calung* plays only alternate pitches of the *pokok*, while the large *jejogan* plays only every fourth pitch. This texture, in which one part simultaneously plays a decorated version of another part, is often described as **heterophony**. Although parts are sometimes slightly varied, essentially they form **ostinati**, particularly in the frequent repetitions of the 'B' sections.

Structure   The excerpt consists of an introduction in free time performed on the *kendhang*. The player sets the tempo and cues features such as repeats and the starts of new sections.

The *ugal* then introduces the core melody, which is simultaneously outlined by the other balungan instruments. Drums, cymbals and *panususan* instruments enter for the loud *angsel* section, after which the music contines with alternations of (and variations on) these two patterns, between which the shorter sections marked 'kendhang accents' offer contrast by featuring mainly drums and the simpler versions of the core melody.

Notice how almost all *gongan* sections end with most instruments coming together on note 6, emphasising the importance of the end accent in gamelan music. This can also be seen in the way that instruments come together on pitch 2 to mark the end of a *keteg*, and in the position of the main notes of the core melody (pitches 1, 2, 5 and 6) which are all played by the *calung* (doubled by the *suling*) on what in western music would be regarded as weak beats.

Exercise 12

1. What is a metallophone?

2. Explain what is meant by a colotomic structure.

3. What is meant by (i) a heterophonic texture and (ii) a *pokok* or nuclear melody?

4. Explain how the function of the gongs differs from the function of panususan instruments such as the small metallophones in this piece.

5. What two features are heard at the end of every *gongan* in *Baris Melampahan*?

6. What was the original function of gamelan music in Indonesia?

Sample questions

In Section B of the Unit 6 paper there will be three questions on pieces from the Applied Music area of study, of which you will have to answer two. Here are three to use for practice.

You can write in continuous prose or short note form. You will be allowed to refer to an unmarked copy of NAM, and you should give the location of each specific feature that you mention. Aim to complete each question in 20 minutes.

(a) Which features of the *Sonata pian' e forte* by Giovanni Gabrieli (NAM 14 pages 194–199) look back to styles of the Renaissance, and which would have sounded more forward-looking when the work was published in 1597?

(b) Cantata No. 48, *Ich elender Mensch*: movements I–IV by Bach (NAM 28, pages 288–299) was written for performance as part of a solemn church service. Identify features of the music that make it particularly appropriate for that purpose. A translation of the text is given on page 538 of NAM.

(c) Jerry Goldsmith was famous for the modern style of his music for *Planet of the Apes*. Identify features of NAM 44 (pages 388–408) that reveal a novel approach to tonality and use of instruments.

Set works for 2014

If you are taking A2 Music in summer 2014, you have to study the seven pieces of instrumental music *below*, plus the five pieces of applied music in the section starting on page 106.

Instrumental music

The pieces for this area of study span musical periods from the early Baroque to the early 20th century:

1550	1600	1650	1700	1750	1800	1850	1900	1950	2000
Renaissance		Baroque			Classical	Romantic		Modern	

Sweelinck *NAM 20* 1615   Bach *NAM 1* c.1721   Beethoven *NAM 17* 1799   Schumann *NAM 23* 1838   Debussy *NAM 24* 1894   Ellington *NAM 49* 1927   Webern *NAM 8* 1930

Pavana Lachrimae (Sweelinck)

Among the most popular types of instrumental music in Elizabethan England were sets of variations on dance tunes or songs. Of the many new songs composed around 1600, Dowland's *Flow my tears* (NAM 33) was perhaps the most famous. Dowland himself wrote variations on it, as did his fellow Englishmen Byrd and Farnaby. All three entitled these works *Pavana Lachrimae* for two reasons. Firstly the song is in the style of a slow processional dance of the late Renaissance known as a pavane. Secondly *Lachrimae* (meaning tears) refers to the image of falling tears with which the words of Dowland's song begins.

A number of English composers, including Dowland, travelled and worked in northern Europe at this time. John Bull, who had earlier been organist of the Chapel Royal in London, was appointed to Antwerp Cathedral and while in the Netherlands became a friend of Sweelinck (organist at the Old Church in Amsterdam for more than 40 years). There can be little doubt that Bull introduced Sweelinck to Dowland's lute songs and the variations written on them by English composers.

Sweelinck's *Pavana Lachrimae* was composed in about 1615 but was not published in the composer's lifetime. The manuscript was probably used as teaching material to be played on the harpsichord (or possibly the organ) by Sweelinck's many pupils.

The work follows the structure of Dowland's song but instead of a repeat of each of its three sections there is a variation. The printed note values of *Flow my tears* are doubled in the *Pavana*, which means that:

➤ Bars 1–8 of the song = bars 1–16 of the pavane

➤ Bars 9–16 of the song = bars 33–48 of the pavane

➤ Bars 17–24 of the song = bars 65–81 of the pavane.

Context

NAM 20 (page 245)	CD2 Track 9
Peter Seymour (harpsichord)	

Structure

Bars			
1–16	A	Dowland bars 1–8
17–32	A^1	Variation on A
33–48	B	Dowland bars 9–16
49–64	B^1	Variation on B
65–81	C	Dowland bars 17–24
82–98	C^1	Variation on C

The example *below* shows the first phrase of Dowland's melody in its original note values and Sweelinck's free transcription of it:

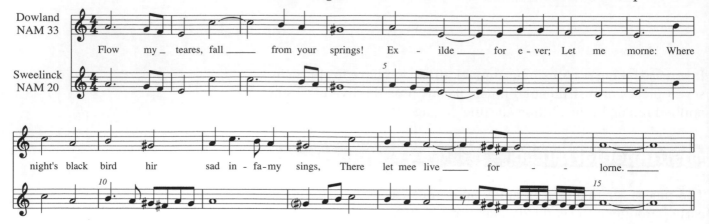

Sweelinck leaves Dowland's harmonies mainly unchanged in these bars, including the **false relation** between G (bass) and G♯ (treble) in bar 10, but he embellishes the cadences in bars 7–8 (left-hand part) and 14–16 (right hand).

You won't be asked questions about Dowland's song in the exam, but comparing NAM 20 with NAM 33 is a good way to understand Sweelinck's variation technique.

Figural variations

At bar 17, instead of repeating the first part of the song to new words, as Dowland did, Sweelinck writes a variation on it, in which mainly **stepwise** semiquavers replace the longer notes of the vocal melody, bass and sometimes an inner part. The constant use of elaborate rhythmic figures to decorate the original has led to this technique being called 'figural variation'. Here we can see how, in bars 17–20, Sweelinck retains all of the pitches of the melody of bars 1–4 within his figural variation:

Sweelinck's variations are mainly of just the melody, but in bar 18 the bass shares the melodic interest by repeating the treble of the previous bar (with one slight change). The same technique is used in bar 24 where the middle 'voice' is allowed a moment of glory.

The remainder of the pavane follows a similar pattern: first a free transcription of eight bars of the song (forming 16 bars in NAM 20 due to the longer note values) and then a variation on it in a more keyboard-like style, forming the structure AA¹BB¹CC¹.

Tonality and harmony

Sweelinck's harmony follows that of Dowland and shows the lingering influence of Renaissance modality. While there are cadences in A minor at the end of each four-bar phrase in the first 16-bar section, the first three are modal-sounding **phrygian cadences** (IVb–V) and the fourth is a perfect cadence with the characteristic **tierce de Picardie** of the late Renaissance style.

Even the brief visit to G major in bars 9–10 sounds quite modal compared with the modulations to closely-related keys that are a feature of later tonal styles (as we shall see in the next work that we study). And in the G-major chord at the start of bar 10, the G♮s in the bass and alto parts are immediately contradicted in the second half of the bar by the G♯s in the melody – such **false relations** are another feature of Renaissance modality. The most pungent example of this device is the simultaneous false relation in bar 96 where the treble G♮ (the highest note in the pavane) sounds against the sustained G♯ on the bass stave.

The majority of chords in NAM 20 are root-position triads and most of the rest are triads in first inversion. The only dissonances that occur on minim beats are **suspensions**, such as those on the second of each pair of tied notes in bars 89–92. Both of these features are typical of late Renaissance styles.

Texture

The sections transcribed from Dowland's song (A, B and C) are mainly in four voice-like parts – the ranges correspond to those of soprano, alto, tenor and bass voices, and the melodic lines move largely by step or by small intervals. Most of these passages are in free **counterpoint**, with occasional imitative entries – for example, compare the soprano part in bars 3–4 with the alto part that started two crotchets earlier. More concentrated imitation occurs in bars 42–45, where the initial four-note figure in the soprano is imitated by bass (with a longer first note), tenor, then by the soprano followed by the bass again, and finally by the alto.

The actual variations (A[1], B[1] and C[1]) are in a much more idiomatic keyboard style. For instance, the semiquaver figuration that starts in the bass of bar 28 rises through almost two and a half octaves to a top D in the right hand of bar 30, and Sweelinck often alternates between three- and four-part textures in these sections.

In the Renaissance, much instrumental music was little different in style to vocal music. By 1600, some of the first truly idiomatic instrumental writing was appearing. This most commonly for keyboard instruments, which could play rapid figuration over a wide range of notes. On CD2, NAM 20 is played on the harpsichord, but it could be played on the virginals (a small, early relative of the harpsichord) or even the organ.

Passages such as that in bars 17–19, where almost identical melodies are heard in the soprano, then the bass, and then the soprano again are not contrapuntal because the other parts merely provide accompaniment. However, Sweelinck introduces a short **canon** towards the end, where the soprano part starting in bar 91[3] is imitated exactly by the bass a compound 4th lower in bar 92 (with the first note split into two crotchets an octave apart).

Exercise 1

1. What sort of dance is a pavane?

2. Why was English music so well known in northern Europe at this time?

3. Explain what is meant by idiomatic keyboard writing and give an example of it from NAM 20.

4. On the first beat of bar 73 the tenor B clashes with the bass C, a major 7th below. What is this type of dissonance called?

5. Using the correct terminology, describe as precisely as you can the cadences in (a) bars 62[3]–64 and (b) bars 96–98.

6. Listen to the recording and describe how the harpsichordist plays the opening chord. Can you spot any other types of ornamentation he uses in the performance?

Bach, *Brandenburg* Concerto No. 4 in G: movement 1

This is a movement from a **concerto grosso** – a type of work popular in the late Baroque period, in which musical material is shared between a small group of soloists (called the **concertino**) and the full orchestra (called the **ripieno**).

In this work, the concertino consists of a solo violin and two solo treble recorders and the ripieno consists of a string ensemble with parts for two violins, viola, cello and double bass. Most of these ripieno parts are usually each played by several performers.

As in most Baroque music, an accompaniment is played by a **continuo** group (so called, because they play almost continuously) consisting of at least one bass instrument (such as a cello) plus at least one harmony instrument (such as a harpsichord or lute). The latter improvises harmonies in accordance with the conventions of the time and guided by any figuring given in the bass part.

There is a clear distinction between the virtuoso solo violin part and the less taxing recorder parts. The violin is given long, sparsely accompanied solos (bars 83–102, for instance), but the recorders nearly always work together, often in **parallel 3rds or 6ths**. This distinction is most noticeable in the extrovert violin solo in bars 187–209, where the recorders supply unobtrusive accompaniment figures in 6ths and 3rds (bars 187–192) that are little different from the duet for ripieno violins in the next six bars.

Instrumentation and scoring

NAM 1 (page 7)   CD1 Track 1
Northern Sinfonia of England
Directed by George Malcolm

This recording uses flutes instead of recorders. Look on *YouTube* for performances that use recorders.

There is no **figured bass** shown in the score of NAM 1, but an example from another work by Bach can be seen on page 288 of NAM.

Context

Bach's six *Brandenburg* concertos were probably written for the small court orchestra of Cöthen, one of the many states into which Germany was then divided, and where Bach was director of music from 1717 to 1723. He subsequently presented a score of the works to the ruler of the much larger state of Brandenburg, hence their title. It is not known if the concertos were ever played at Brandenburg, but most were forgotten after Bach's death in 1750. Even after the rediscovery of Bach's manuscripts in the 19th century performances were rare. It was not until the 20th century, when recording made the *Brandenburg* concertos available to a wide audience, that these works became established as some of the best-loved instrumental music of the Baroque period.

Brandenburg Concerto No. 4 is modelled on the type of concerto that was perfected by the Italian composer Vivaldi, who was just seven years older than Bach. Bach studied Vivaldi's concertos by making his own arrangements of them. One of the most famous is Vivaldi's Concerto Op. 3, No. 8 – a concerto grosso for two violins and strings that Bach transcribed as a work for organ alone.

Rhythm and metre

As in most of Bach's instrumental music – and much of his sacred music too – dance rhythms are clearly in evidence. The unvarying one-in-a-bar triple metre is enlivened by the syncopated rhythms of the recorders in bars 4, 6, 15, 17, 43–47 and so on, and by **hemiolas** (the *basso continuo* in bars 80–81 effectively goes into one bar of $\frac{3}{4}$ time, as shown *left*). These bars contain the most joyful and complex rhythms of the whole movement. The upper strings accentuate the second, first then the third quavers of each bar (and are therefore out of phase with the bass hemiola), while

the recorders accentuate the intervening quavers (and are therefore in phase with it). But all of the parts agree on the characteristic syncopated rhythm at the cadence, where the second quaver of bar 82 gets particular emphasis because the chords change at this point (IV^7–V^7). Bach uses this startling collection of syncopations elsewhere in the movement, always to signal the end of an important section, thus underlining the structure of the music.

Listen to the movement and try to work out how it is put together. It starts with a long opening section (bars 1–83) that begins with a I–V–I chord progression heard four times in the first 12 bars in order to firmly establish the tonic key of G major. This first section ends with syncopated rhythms and a perfect cadence in bars 79–83. Listen to the recording without the score, but use these two features as markers in order to identify what happens in the rest of the music.

Did you notice that, between the solo sections, parts of the opening music return in different keys, and that all of the opening music is repeated in the tonic key at the end? This is known as **ritornello form**. Ritornello means 'a little return' and it refers to a structure in which shortened repetitions are sandwiched between contrasting sections called **episodes**). It is a musical form that was widely used for long movements in the Baroque period. This structure is summarised in the table *right* – we have given timings since this may help you follow the music without needing to use the score. Only the main keys, which are all close relatives of the tonic, G major, are shown in this table.

The solo episodes do not stay in one key. Instead they modulate from the key of the previous ritornello to the key of the next. Notice how small fragments of the ritornello punctuate these sections, as in bars 89–91. Because this fragment consists of the progression I–V–I Bach can use it as a perfect cadence to highlight the most important keys through which the music passes, as in bars 103–105, where they appear in the dominant, D major. However the orchestra mainly takes a background role during the solo episodes, as can be seen in the sustained A in bars 125–128. Sometimes the accompaniment is provided by just the continuo. Listen to the harpsichordist's improvisation starting at bar 114 and say how this relates to the violin solo that it accompanies.

Bach's melodic lines often include arpeggio figures that outline the underlying chords. For example, the second recorder's arpeggios in bars 1–2 clearly trace the triads played by *ripieno* strings (chords I and V). Variants are two-a-penny: for instance, a triad of E minor is as clear in the upper string parts in bar 14 as it is in the second recorder's arpeggio in the same bar. Such harmonically charged melodic lines are particularly obvious in the extended violin solos. For instance, the unaccompanied violin in bar 84 clearly changes the G-major triad of bar 83 into the dominant seventh of C major. Even when Bach writes scale-based figures, as in bars 187–208, the harmonic implications are almost as clear. For instance, in bar 202 the violin part changes the underlying G major triad into the dominant 7th of C major and so initiates the lead into C major for the third ritornello (bars 209–235).

Structure and tonality

When reading the score, note that the viola part is written in the alto clef, in which the middle line represents middle C.

Bars	Structure	Key	Timing
1–83	Ritornello 1	G	0:00
83–137	Episode 1	G→D	1:23
137–157	Ritornello 2	E mi	2:14
157–209	Episode 2	E mi	2:36
209–235	Ritornello 3	C	3:28
235–323	Episode 3	C	3:55
323–344	Ritornello 4	B mi	5:21
345–427	Ritornello 1	G	5:44

Melody and motif

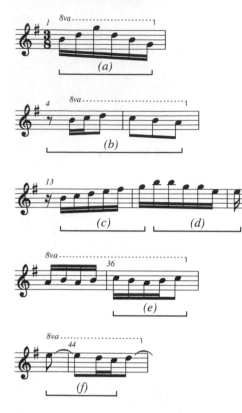

(a)

(b)

(c)   (d)

(e)

(f)

Some of these melodic figures are more important than others since they are seeds from which long melodic passages later flower, often by sequential development but sometimes merely by repetition. Motif *(a)*, shown *left*, is immediately repeated a 4th lower to form a sequence in bars 1–2, followed in bar 3 by the last three quavers of motif *(b)*. Bars 4–6 consist of the whole of motif *(b)* plus a sequence of its first four notes overlapping the start of a repeat of the first six bars in bars 7–12.

Motifs *(c)* and *(d)* come from the violin solo that starts in bar 13. Bach develops these into an extended melody that begins with a rising sequence built out of both motifs. Then, in bars 18–22, a descending sequence is built out of motif *(d)* alone. This organic growth of a melody from the seeds of mere motifs is called *Fortspinnung* in German. It means 'spinning-out' and the process is typical of late-Baroque melodies.

There are just two other motifs, labelled *(e)* and *(f) left*. Sometimes *(e)* is preceded by four semiquavers, but more often it appears on its own. Look at the first recorder part that begins in bar 35. Motif *(e)* is first heard in bar 36 and is attached by a tie to a varied repetition of itself in bar 37. Bars 38–39 contain an inversion of motif *(c)* and this leads to a sequential repetition of the whole phrase in bars 40–43, at which point motif *(f)* first appears. This syncopated motif is twice repeated in a descending sequence (bars 43–47). Simultaneously the continuo, solo violin and ripieno violin parts provide counter-melodies fashioned out of motif *(d)*.

In almost every bar of this movement one or more of the melodic strands derive from these six motifs: together they provide the thematic glue that holds the structure together.

Harmony

> **Functional harmony** refers to the use of chord progressions, particularly cadences, that establish the main key(s) of a work, and which thus help to give it structure.

Much of the movement is built on triads in root position and first inversion. The harmony is **functional** and mostly **diatonic**, with chord changes (or at least an octave leap in the bass) at each barline.

Chords I and V$^{(7)}$ in root position are particularly important in this movement. We have already seen that they are the only chords used in the first 12 bars, and perfect cadences (V$^{(7)}$–I) in various keys are used frequently throughout the music.

> In a circle of 5ths, alternate intervals rise a 4th instead of descending a 5th (the harmonic effect is the same) since a literal succession of descending 5ths would take the part below the range of most bass instruments.

Other progressions in which the roots of chords fall in 5ths are also important, particularly **circles of 5ths**, such as that in bars 79–80 where the bass notes are B–E–A–D–G–C (see *below*). The whole progression in bars 79–83 is typical of this movement in its diatonic simplicity, in its reliance on mainly root-position chords and in the faster rate of chord change at the approach to a cadence (compare the following with bars 75–78, in which there is only one chord per bar):

Ib VI II   V I IV IIb Ic VI IV^7 V V^7 I

Similar progressions, consisting of a circle of 5ths, a hemiola and a perfect cadence, occur in various related keys at the end of each ritornello.

Bach generally uses a 'pivot chord' to smooth the modulation to a new key. For example, the chord of E minor in bar 14 is chord VI in the key we are leaving (G major) and chord II in the key we are approaching (D major).

Sometimes the harmony is a little more complex. Look at bar 22, where the recorders outline a chord of A^7 followed by a chord of D in bar 23. Under the A^7 in bar 22, the bass instruments outline a triad of D major. This strange combination of tonic and dominant harmony is the result of Bach's relentless pursuit of the sequence of one-bar units begun by the solo violin in bar 18, then imitated in the bass starting in bar 20.

Chromatic chords are rare, apart from the **Neapolitan 6th** which Bach uses, for example, at the start of bar 155 (before a cadence in E minor) and at bar 341 (before a cadence in B minor).

Most dissonances in the movement arise from the frequent use of **passing notes** and **auxiliary notes**, but the tempo is too fast for these (or even the occasional **accented passing notes**) to make any noticeable impact. Equally familiar in the late Baroque style are the **anticipations** which occur immediately before the final chord of each of the main cadences (for example, the semiquaver G above a chord of D major in the 1st violin and 1st recorder parts of bar 426, which anticipates the G in the final bar of the movement). **Suspensions**, though, are a distinctive part of the style – a long chain of them occurs in bars 165–184 (look for the tied notes).

Sequences abound in this late Baroque style. Bars 35^2–39^1 (V–I in G) are repeated in bars 39^2–43^1 to create a modulating sequence (V–I in C). This is immediately followed by a descending diatonic sequence – look at the pattern of falling 3rds in the bass that starts on the second quaver of bar 43 and that progressively steps down the scale (C–A–F♯, B–G–E, A–F♯–D and G–E–C).

Texture

Bach was (and still is) famed for his skill in writing **contrapuntal** textures. These include:

➢ Four-part counterpoint (the three independent *concertino* parts over a walking bass) in bars 13–22

➢ Recorders in 3rds and 6ths (and later in imitation with each other) in counterpoint with the violin melody of bars 35–58

➢ Two freely imitative parts above a walking bass (bars 165–184)

➢ An accompanied **canon** (between ripieno violin 1 and recorder 1 at the distance of a quaver) that is heard simultaneously with elaborate solo violin passagework in bars 198–208

➢ Three solo parts in close canon over a tonic pedal in C major (starting at bar 235 and repeated in G, starting at bar 251).

Textures change frequently in the movement and not all are contrapuntal. The opening bars are **homophonic**, and the big gap between melody and bass in bars 4–6 (which can be filled by the harpsichord) is known as a **polarised texture**. There are brief **monophonic** passages (e.g. bars 84, 86 and 88) and **antiphonal exchanges** between pairs of instruments in bars 257–263.

Exercise 2

1. Name one chordal instrument and one bass instrument that might play a continuo part.

2. Explain the difference between the ripieno and the concertino.

3. In ritornello form, what is the name for the passages heard *between* the main ritornello sections?

4. In bar 1, which note of a G-major triad is played by the violas – is it the root, 3rd or 5th of the chord?

5. In bar 388, the recorders play the notes C and E above a chord of D major. What is this harmonic device called?

6. Explain how the music of bar 388 is treated in bars 389 and 390.

7. What is meant by a Neapolitan 6th? State the number of a bar in which Bach uses this chord.

Septet in E♭: movement 1 (Beethoven)

Context

NAM 17 (page 207) CD2 Track 6
Berlin Philharmonic Octet

A septet is a type of **chamber music** for seven solo players. This particular example is on a relatively large scale, consisting of six movements (of which NAM 17 is the first). Beethoven wrote the work at the end of 1799 and it received its first public performance in April 1800 at a concert in the Royal Imperial Court Theatre, Vienna, where it shared the programme with the premiere of his first symphony. The Septet was well received and it proved to be Beethoven's most popular work for some years to come. Note that:

➤ The clarinet in B♭ sounds a tone lower than printed

➤ The horn in E♭ sounds a major 6th lower than printed (the horn did not have valves at this time, and so could produce only a limited selection of pitches)

➤ The double bass sounds an octave lower than printed.

Introduction

The movement begins with a slow introduction that moves from the opening tonic chord of E♭ major to chord V in bar 8 (preceded by a German **augmented 6th** chord in bar 7). Notice the dramatic contrast between the loud **tutti** opening and the solo violin figures. The four violin notes starting after the rest in bar 8 will dominate much of the rest of the movement. Bars 8–10 are repeated in the tonic minor (E♭ minor, bars 10–12). The major mode returns for the ornate violin melody that ends on a dominant-7th chord (bars 17–18), decorated with a very characteristic clarinet arpeggio.

Sonata form

The *Allegro con brio* that follows the introduction is in sonata form, the most common structure for first movements in the Classical period, just as ritornello form was the most common structure for long movements in the Baroque period. It is based on the idea of juxtaposing the tonic key with a related key (usually the dominant or relative major) in the first section – often with contrasting themes in each key, as occurs here. Tonal conflict becomes more apparent in the middle section, in which the thematic material is developed through a wider range of keys, but this conflict is resolved in the final section, which is centred entirely on the tonic key:

Bars	18		53		111		154		188		233	
	Exposition				Development		Recapitulation				Coda	
	1st subject		2nd subject				1st subject	2nd subject				
Keys	E♭ major		B♭ major		Various		E♭ major		E♭ major		E♭ major	

Exposition

The first subject starts with a version of the four-note motif we noticed in the introduction, treated in **sequence** in bars 18–21. The whole of the ten-bar violin melody is repeated on the clarinet, supported by a **syncopated** accompaniment in the strings.

The harmony is generally simple and **diatonic**, although decorated with chromatic notes such as those in bar 26. The **harmonic rhythm** is often slow, speeding up towards the cadences. This is evident in the first subject (bars 18–29) in which the first four bars are all harmonised with chord I, then the chords change every bar in bars 23–26, then every half bar in the next two bars.

The second subject, which starts at bar 53 in the dominant key of B♭ major, initially has a very different character: a **homophonic** texture of three-part strings, at first in minims although when this four-bar phrase is repeated by wind (bars 57–60) the violin adds lively quavers. Another second subject theme in bars 61–68 is shared between violin and clarinet doubled by bassoon, the start of which is then immediately repeated in a different scoring. Finally Beethoven introduces a third idea (also part of the second subject) – the staccato chordal phrase in bars 86–88. This is repeated in sequence and (in bars 90–92) at the original pitch but with varied harmony. A **cadential** $\frac{6}{4}$ (in the typically Classical progression Ic–V–I) concludes the second subject in bars 97–98.

Bars 98^3–111 form a **codetta** that reinforces the dominant key (B♭ major). The melody for clarinet and bassoon (bars 98^3–100^2) is based on the opening notes of the first subject and is repeated in sequence (bars 100^3–102^2), and then varied by the violin, over a reiterated tonic pedal (B♭ played by horn then double bass). The exposition ends with three perfect cadences (bars 107–111).

Development

The development of ideas from the exposition begins with the four-note motif from the opening of the first subject and a rapid modulation to C minor. In this key the melody from the codetta is heard on the clarinet (bars 116–120). The same theme is then heard in sequence on the horn and the music starts to modulate through a wider range of keys, as is usual in a development section.

At bar 125 Beethoven draws on another earlier idea (from bar 40) which alternates with the codetta theme until a dominant pedal in bar 140 heralds the imminent return of the tonic key. Over the pedal the codetta theme is combined with a new version of the minim motif from bar 53. Our four-note motif then appears in rising sequence (bars 148–151), climbing up a chord of V^7 (cello in **dialogue** with viola and woodwind).

Recapitulation

The recapitulation starts with a rescored repeat of bars 18–30, but a sudden modulation to A♭ major in bars 166–172 leads to more development of earlier material until, at bar 182, Beethoven returns to E♭ major for a repeat of bars 47–98 in the tonic key.

Coda   The **coda** begins at bar 233 with a repeat of the codetta, but it is greatly expanded by further development of the four-note motif (starting in the cello at bar 249). This accompanies a variation of the codetta theme played on the horn, together with a syncopated dominant pedal on the violin. At bar 258 the two melodies swap positions, the four-note motif now in the treble and the codetta theme in the bass, the latter imitated by woodwind in bar 260. Arpeggios and scales lead to a conclusive cadence in E♭ major (bars 276–277). The movement ends with a new trill figure, compressed in rhythm to increase excitement from bar 285, and harmonised by no fewer than nine perfect cadences in the last 11 bars.

Texture   One of the features that made this work so popular when it first appeared is its lively variety of texture. Let's choose some of the most diverse passages and describe them as concisely as possible.

➤ Bars 1–4: tutti chords flank the **monophonic** texture of bar 2

➤ Bars 8–11: alternation of three-part strings and tutti chords

➤ Bars 12–14: melody-dominated **homophony** (tune in violin accompanied by wind and cello, with melodic fragments in the viola)

➤ Bars 47–49: an **antiphonal exchange** between wind and strings

➤ Bars 111–115: melody in octaves with harmony sketched in by horn and double bass

➤ Bars 221^3–231^1: a **homorhythmic** texture in which three-part string chords alternate with tutti chords

➤ Bars 254–257: two-part **counterpoint** (clarinet and horn in octaves against lower strings in octaves) plus a tonic pedal in bassoon and violin

➤ Bars 258–264: **imitation** (the part for cello and bass is imitated by oboe and bassoon in bar 260, which in turn is imitated by cello and bass in bar 262) plus a **countermelody** for violin. The violin and bass parts in bars 258–261 form a contrapuntal inversion of the clarinet and bass parts in the previous four bars

➤ Bars 274–277: a duet for clarinet and bassoon above sustained string chords.

Style   This movement reflects many of the features of the Classical style that can also be heard in the mature works of Haydn and Mozart as well as in the music of Beethoven:

➤ The inclusion of instruments that were still relatively new at this time, such as the clarinet and horn, and the abandonment of a continuo part

➤ A preference for homophonic textures and antiphonal exchanges between instruments, with less use of counterpoint

➤ Dramatic contrasts in dynamics and many more performance markings in the score than were used in earlier periods

➤ A vocabulary of mainly diatonic chords, decorated with melodic chromaticism (and with occasional chromatic chords, such as the German augmented 6ths on C♭ in bars 7 and 248)

➤ Clear cadences that define keys: in particular, the cadential $^6_4$ (the first chord in the progression Ic–V–I, in bars 28–29, 38–39, 97–98 etc.) is one of the fingerpints of the Classical style

➤ **Periodic phrasing** created by pairs of equal-length phrases that sound like questions and answers (for example, the four-bar clarinet phrase in bars 116–120 ends with a perfect cadence in C minor and is answered by a four-bar horn phrase in bars 120–124 that ends with a balancing perfect cadence in A♭ major).

Exercise 3

1. Name the pitches *sounded* in bar 1 by (i) the clarinet, and (ii) the horn.

2. Compare bars 2 and 4.

3. In bars 161–164 the key is E♭ major. Which of these bars are diatonic and which include chromatic writing?

4. What is the name of the ornament in the violin part of bar 163?

5. What precisely is meant by 'a syncopated dominant pedal' in the description of the coda, *opposite*?

6. Compare bars 53–56 with bars 188–191. What is the main difference between these two passages?

7. To what extent are the cello and double bass parts independent in this movement?

8. Which two instruments have most of the melodic interest in NAM 17?

9. Give an example of **double-stopping** on page 207 of NAM.

Kinderscenen: Nos. 1, 3 and 11 (Schumann)

The Romantic period in music was an age of extremes, with works ranging from opera, choral and orchestral music on a huge scale, through extremely difficult solo music for virtuoso professionals, to modest songs and piano pieces for amateurs to enjoy at home.

The set of musical miniatures for the piano entitled *Kinderscenen* (Scenes of Childhood), written by the German composer Robert Schumann in 1838, was clearly designed for the domestic market. Works of this type are called character pieces (or characteristic pieces) and are intended to express intense emotional experiences in the most intimate manner. They were extremely popular – Romantic composers could hardly keep up with the demand.

Although Schumann wrote the music first and gave each of the 13 pieces an individual title later, he always intended *Kinderscenen* to be a set of reminiscences of childhood that would be played by adults, unlike his *Album for the Young*, written for his seven-year-old daughter (and for all young pianists) to play.

Schumann's titles deliberately encourage us, as we listen or play, to allow memories to float across our minds: images of distant lands and people, a game of blind man's bluff and spooky childhood experiences. These programmatic interpretations are typical of much Romantic music and are quite different from the

Context

NAM 23 (page 258) CD2 Tracks 13–15
Alfred Brendel (piano)

earlier pieces we have studied, in which the composers made no suggestions about how their music should be experienced. Pieces with titles such as concerto or septet are sometimes described as absolute music. They don't tell a story or paint a scene, but instead depend upon purely musical ideas that can be enjoyed in as abstract a fashion as the listener wishes.

Even more characteristic of early Romanticism is the fragmentary, suggestive nature of many of the pieces in *Kinderscenen*. Thus the melody of 'Von fremden Ländern und Menschen' ends inconclusively on the mediant rather than the tonic, and the accompaniment runs on through the final bar, as though the pianist had intended to stop but instead drifted off into a romantic daydream.

The reverse happens in 'Fürchtenmachen' in which the music slides in as though it had been going for some time and had only just become audible. This effect is enhanced by the chromatic writing in the first two bars which disguises the tonic key.

Von fremden Ländern und Menschen

The first eight bars are repeated at the end, after a six-bar middle section, forming the pattern ‖:A:‖:BA:‖ which is known as **rounded binary form**. Binary because the double barlines divide the piece into two sections, and rounded because the second section (B) is rounded off by a return of the opening material (A).

The melody is simple, repetitive and entirely **diatonic** – features reflecting the style of the innocent German folk songs that so pleased the growing middle classes of the early Romantic period. But while the many repetitions of the opening two-bar phrase and the short **sequence** in bars 9–12 give the impression of a children's song, this is an adult's recollection of childhood. Therefore, do not be surprised by sophisticated chromatic harmonies such as the diminished-7th chord in bars 1 and 3, the juxtaposition of the unrelated triads of B major and G major in bar 12, and the artful left-hand **countermelody** based on a **circle of 5ths** in bars 9–12.

Schumann's piano textures are also far from childlike. Notice the way the broken chords are shared between the hands, the contrast between the legato melody and semi-staccato bass at the start, the two-part **counterpoint** between the outer parts in bars 9–14, and subtle nuances such as the sustained notes in inner parts (bars 5–6 and 14). Other points to note are:

➢ Balanced **periodic phrasing** (2+2+4 bars in the first section, shown by the phrase marks) – typical of Schumann's style but also typical of music from the preceding Classical period (as we saw in NAM 17)

➢ An A section that does not modulate and that is repeated almost exactly when it returns in bars 15–22

➢ A central B section (bars 9–14) that is melodically distinct from section A and that makes only fleeting reference to a different key (E minor)

➢ Triplet figuration in the middle part that continues throughout the piece.

The combination of a simple diatonic melody with subtle and sometimes ambiguous harmonic touches, in a texture of **melody-dominated homophony**, is typical of Schumann in his dreamy romantic mode. The effect is enhanced by the frequent rhythmic blurring caused when the dotted patterns coincide with triplets, often tempting the performer to use **rubato** (encouraged by the ritardando followed by a pause in bars 12–14).

By 1838 the piano could be found in middle-class homes throughout western Europe, and Schumann's idiomatic writing exploits some of its most characteristic features. The **articulation** of the uppermost part as a song-like melody depends on the performer's ability to play it more loudly than the lower parts (despite the fact that the highest notes of the accompaniment must be played with the right-hand thumb). It also depends on the type of mellow tone that was possible as piano manufacturers increasingly chose to cover the instrument's hammers with felt rather than leather.

Schumann's romantic style also relies on the sustaining power of pianos with iron (rather than wooden) frames, which were becoming popular by now, and on the careful use of the sustaining pedal. The artful two-part counterpoint between the outer parts in bars 9–14, with continued harmonic filling, is typical of Romantic textures that are enhanced by the sustaining power that pianos had achieved by this time. Nevertheless, none of these pieces explores the highest or lowest ranges of the piano, perhaps underlining the fact that they were intended for the domestic market rather than for the concert hall.

Hasche-Mann

This is another rounded binary-form (with a written-out repeat of the first four bars) and with tell-tale signs of Romanticism, such as the sudden intrusion of C major into the key of B minor in bars 13–15. Once again a constant rhythm, this time semiquavers, is heard in one part or another right through to the final bar.

The game of blind-man's bluff ('Catch me if you can') is evoked by scurrying semiquavers. The first two bars are repeated in sequence, creating a four-bar phrase which is then repeated in bars 5–8. Like the A section of 'Von fremden Ländern', these bars never move out of the tonic key (in this case B minor). The prominent flattened leading note (A♮) in bar 2 comes from the use of the descending melodic minor scale, but A♯ appears in the perfect cadences (V^7–I in B minor) in bars 4 and 8.

The rising sequence of bars 1–4 is balanced by a falling sequence in bars 9–12, carrying the music to the unrelated key of C major. Clearly-defined tonal centres are avoided through the use of interrupted cadences in G major (bars 10–11) and E minor (bars 12–13). Like a disorientated, blindfolded child, the music seems to get stuck on a chord of C (bars 13–15). Indeed, we seem to be in the key of C major judging by the alternating C and G^7 chords above the double pedal on C and G. But in bars 15–17 the tonic key is regained by the appearance of chords V^7 and I of B minor, the home key.

The texture is again melody-dominated homophony, with a difficult leaping accompaniment for the left hand to suggest the jerky, lurching movements of the blindfolded child.

Fürchtenmachen

The ABACABA structure of this piece is known as symmetrical **rondo form**. The A section is called the refrain, while the other sections (B in bars 9–12, repeated in bars 37–40, and C in bars 21–28) are called **episodes**. Both episodes contrast vividly with the refrain and Schumann emphasises this by marking episode B *schneller* (faster) in bars 9 and 37. On CD2 Alfred Brendel sensibly extends this idea to episode C at bar 21.

The refrain consists of two soothing four-bar phrases in G major. Both start with the type of chromatic harmony that disguises the true key and is typical of the Romantic style, but both end with clear imperfect cadences in G major. Notice how, when the opening four-bar melody is freely adapted to form the answering melody of bars 5–8, it starts in the left hand (bar 5) and then transfers to the right hand on the second quaver of bar 7.

Both episodes are characterised by syncopated chords. The first two bars of Episode B are in E minor (the relative minor) and are repeated in sequence a third lower (in C major, but ending on an ambiguous second-inversion chord of E minor).

There is no clear tonal centre in the second episode (C) – the shifting chromaticism gives it an unsettling effect which is part of Schumann's hazy recollection of childhood fear. In fact, the 'scare' seems to be no more than a brief flash-back, since the new rhythm pattern, off-beat *sforzandi* and loud dynamic all vaporise after four bars. The remainder of the episode then wends its way back to the soothing mood of the refrain, while Schumann cleverly avoids an exact sequence when bars 25–26 are varied to form bars 27–28.

Many of the cadences are imperfect, and when Schumann uses a perfect cadence, the tonic chord is often placed on a weaker beat that the dominant (as in bar 24^2 and bar 48).

Further examples of Schumann's idiomatic piano writing can be seen in his use of a bass melody with right-hand accompaniment in bars 5–6 and 9–12, and in the sudden contrast of dynamic and the off-beat accents in bars 21–24.

Exercise 4

1. Name the main key of each of the three pieces in NAM 23.

2. What term is often used to describe short Romantic piano pieces of this type?

3. Describe the texture and form of 'Von fremden Ländern und Menschen' using appropriate technical terms.

4. What type of scale occurs in bar 16 of 'Hasche-Mann'?

5. What does diatonic mean?

6. In a rondo, what is the difference between an episode and the refrain?

7. Explain what is meant by idiomatic instrumental writing, and give three examples of ways in which Schumann's piano pieces in NAM 23 are idiomatic.

8. Which features of the music suggest that *Kinderscenen* was intended for adults, not children, to play?

Sarabande from *Pour le piano* (Debussy)

The original version of this Sarabande by the French composer Claude Debussy was written in 1894. He later revised some of the harmonies and included the piece as the middle movement of his suite *Pour le piano* ('for the piano') of 1901, which is the version printed in NAM 24. This suite is one of a number of works composed at the end of the Romantic period by composers such as Grieg, Tchaikovsky and Debussy, that sought to revive and inject new life into 18th-century forms, particularly dances.

The performance direction at the head of the score ('with slow and solemn elegance') captures the stately, triple-time mood of the Baroque sarabande, with its characteristic accent on the second beat of the bar (bar 2, 4, 8 and so on). Also similar to Baroque dance movements (such as those in NAM 21) is the binary structure in which a short A section (bars 1–22) is followed by a longer B section (bars 23–72).

When we listen to the sarabande, though, it is clear that Debussy is not seeking to copy the style of 18th-century music, but merely using some of its features as a springboard for his own ideas.

The work is not written for harpsichord but for piano, and Debussy uses just over five octaves of its complete range, with a preference for the rich tones of the middle and lower registers, particularly noticeable in the sonorous bass notes of the final bars.

As mentioned *above*, Debussy reflects the characteristic second-beat emphasis of the sarabande style by stopping the flow on a minim (bars 2, 4, 8 and so on), or by using a dotted crotchet, tied note or tenuto mark (as in bar 21) on the second beat of the bar. In the first 18 bars this has the effect of dividing the music into two- and four-bar phrases that reflect the style of a dance.

However, as the piece progresses Debussy's phrasing starts to obscure the dance rhythm. This is most obvious in bars 38–41, where the phrasing across the barlines cuts across the triple-time pulse, an effect known as **cross phrasing**. Notice how Debussy beams the notes in an unconventional fashion in order to reflect this cross phrasing.

In bars 67–68 the dance rhythm is again disturbed, this time by the introduction of a **hemiola**. Here Debussy is simply using a rhythmic device found at the approach to cadences in many Baroque sarabandes and in much other triple-time Baroque music, as we know from our study of NAM 1 – although hemiolas then would never have included such dissonant chords as these.

Despite the key signature of C♯ minor, the melody in the first section (bars 1–22) is entirely in the **aeolian mode**. You can find the aeolian mode by playing the white notes on the piano from A to the A an octave higher.

The aeolian mode transposed to C♯, as used by Debussy, is shown *right*. It differs from the scale of C♯ minor in using B(♮) instead of B♯. Note that Debussy keeps us waiting until bar 22 for a cadence on the final ('tonic') of the mode.

Context

| NAM 24 (page 260) CD2 Track 16 |
| Zoltán Kocsis (piano) |

The letters *m.d.* in bar 72 stand for *main droite* (right hand), indicating that the tied chord must be held with the sustaining pedal so that both hands are free for these bass notes.

Rhythm

Melody and harmony

The harmony in the first eight bars is equally modal, with cadences that end with a *minor* triad on the fifth degree of the mode (G♯) in bars 2 and 4, and a major triad on the seventh degree (B) in bar 8. But the streams of gentle discords in bars 1 and 3 draw a misty veil over the modality. Debussy is *not* using **functional harmony** – he is using both concords and discords purely as sound events.

The one-bar melodic fragment in bars 9–10 is accompanied by root position triads containing a false relation effect (A♮/A♯) typical of much 16th and early 17th-century music. But when this melodic fragment is repeated at a lower pitch in bars 11–12, it is accompanied by **parallel 7th chords** which add sensuous colour but that have no tonal function as none of the 7ths resolves. These chords blur the modality of the melody all the more effectively because the bass ascends through five of the six pitches of a **whole-tone scale** (D–E–F♯–G♯ in bars 11 and 12 leading to an A♯ in bar 13). This scale was to become increasingly important in some of Debussy's later works.

The central section (bars 23–41) begins with **quartal harmony** (chords consisting of superimposed 4ths). Then, initially as a result of the two-bar sequences in bars 25–28, **chromaticism** invades both melody and harmony.

When the original melody returns in bar 42 it is re-harmonised with unrelated and chromatic root-position chords, but the second phrase (bars 46–49) returns to the chaste modal harmonies that characterised the first eight bars. Mock-medieval parallel 5ths in the bass of bars 50–53 cover all but one of the modal pitches, but the dissonances formed with the chromatic chords above them help generate the climax of the whole piece – the chord of D♯ major in bar 55. This is the only truly tonal moment in the whole piece: with the *ff* chord in the next bar it forms a perfect cadence in G♯ minor, the dominant of C♯ minor. But when V of G♯ minor returns in the cadence at bar 59 it fails to resolve, simply slumping on to a chord of C♯ minor at the start of bar 60.

In the last six bars, 4th-based chords ascend above a sequence of falling 5ths in the bass (G♯–C♯, B–E, D♯–G♯) and the whole piece finishes with a modal cadence (B rising to C♯ in the melody). Although the sarabande ends on a chord of C♯ minor, there is no sense of a perfect cadence in that key.

Notice that while the piece as a whole makes use of a range of more than five octaves, the range of most melodic phrases is quite narrow, However, Debussy often uses a wider range of notes in phrases that lead to the ends of sections (bars 6–8, 39–41 etc.)

Structure

The form of this sarabande is almost as elusive as its tonality. Baroque dances were usually in binary form and Debussy uses a double barline at the end of bar 22 as if to indicate that this is the dividing point between A and B sections. However, the music ends on C♯, the main tonal centre, in bar 22, whereas the A section of most Baroque binary movements ends in a related key rather than in the home key.

Furthermore, bars 23–41 are more different in style to the first section than would be usual in Baroque binary form and, while the references to the A section from bar 42 onwards might seem to hint at the rounded binary structures we saw in NAM 23, they are too substantial, too much altered and too soon before the end to make a convincing case for rounded binary form.

Some have suggested that the whole piece could be regarded as **ternary form**, with a modified repeat of the first section starting in bar 42. But this 'repeat' starts in the wrong 'key' and there is as much new material here as there is repeated music.

When listening to the sarabande, see if you can hear a **rondo**-like patchwork of repeated sections (all of them significantly varied), in which the first 22 bars form a short **ternary** structure. The entire piece could be represented like this:

> Although having a range of different (but valid) views on the structure of the music may seem confusing, remember that composers don't write with the intention of creating neat answers for students! Examiners will accept any of the suggestions here, providing you justify your views about the structure.

Bars 1–8	9–14	15–22	23–41	42–49	50–55	56–62	63–72
A	B	A¹	C	A²	D	B¹	coda

The final section, or **coda**, begins with four bars centred around the 'dominant' of the mode (G♯) while the remainder leads up through more quartal harmony to the final modal cadence.

What holds this patchwork together is not so much the varied repetitions of sections A and B, but the sarabande rhythm and repetitions of the little figure of two semiquavers and a quaver first heard in bar 9.

Texture

The principal texture is chordal and in some places (such as bars 1–2) all the notes move exactly together to give a **homorhythmic** texture. Most chords are dense and sonorous – notice in particular the massive ten-note chord in bar 53 – and successions of parallel chords, such as those in bars 35–41, form a distinctive element in the texture. Short passages of bare octaves (such as bars 5–6[1] and 20–22) create a dramatic contrast to the very full textures elsewhere in the piece.

Debussy uses a wide range of the instrument (notice the sonorous low melody in bars 20–22 and the final bass notes), and there are passages with both hands in the bass clef (bars 23–26) and both in the treble clef (bars 38–40).

Exercise 5

1. What are the main features of a sarabande?

2. Compare bars 42–49 with bars 1–8.

3. Where is the melody that starts in bar 56 first heard?

4. What term describes the harmony in bars 67–70 of NAM 24?

5. Define the terms hemiola and cross-phrasing, and give an example of each from this sarabande.

6. Explain what is meant by parallel chords and give an example of their use in this sarabande.

7. What is unusual about the final cadence of NAM 24?

8. Which aspects of Debussy's sarabande are new and forward-looking and which are drawn from older types of music?

9. Which note of the scale of C♯ minor is rarely used in this piece, thus making it sound modal?

Black and Tan Fantasy
(Duke Ellington and Bubber Miley)

Context

In 1908, just seven years after the publication of the suite *Pour le piano*, Debussy completed another piano suite, *Children's Corner*, which ends with a cakewalk – a piece that mimicked the popular ragtime music of the day. The highly syncopated style of ragtime was an important ingredient in the development of jazz in the USA during the early decades of the 20th century.

The essence of jazz is improvisation, but as jazz bands became larger during the 1920s and 30s in order to fill ever-larger dance halls with sound, collective improvisation became impractical and at least some of the music had to be composed and notated.

Duke Ellington is one of the few major figures in jazz whose reputation rests more on his compositions and arrangements than his work as a performer. In 1924 he took over the leadership of a small jazz band in New York which he expanded in size and which in 1927 was awarded a contract to play at the Cotton Club, one of the city's leading nightclubs and a venue for frequent radio broadcasts. Although located in the heart of the black community of Harlem it catered for an entirely white audience, who came to see floorshows based on highly stereotyped ideas of African culture. To accompany these, Ellington developed what is known as his jungle style, featuring heavy drums, dark saxophone textures and rough, growling brass sounds, all evident in the *Black and Tan Fantasy*, first recorded in 1927.

Listen to the recording and make sure you can identify the three main sections of Ellington's jazz orchestra:

> Reeds (saxophones and clarinet)

> Brass (trumpets and trombone) and

> A rhythm section of piano, banjo, drums and (double) bass.

Ellington worked closely with his band, adapting his arrangements to the talents of its members and leaving space for their individual solos. He often involved members of the band in the arrangement, as in the *Black and Tan Fantasy*, which was a collaboration between Ellington and his lead trumpeter, Bubber Miley.

Structure

'Black and Tan' refers to venues in Harlem, such as the Cotton Club where Ellington worked, in which black and white people came together, although in a very segregated way (audiences were white, staff were black). A fantasy is a work in which the composer follows his own fancy, rather than a set form, but here Ellington is using the word in its everyday sense to express his own fantasy that racial integration might one day be possible. This duality of meaning is reflected in two unusual aspects of the work, both of which refer to the social commentary implied by the title:

> The opening 12-bar blues (suggesting black-American music) in the key of B♭ minor is immediately followed by a contrasting section of 16 bars in B♭ major (see *left*) that features chromatic harmony – a phrase structure and harmonic style more associated with European music

NAM 49 (page 465)   CD4 Track 8
Duke Ellington and his orchestra

Bars		
1–12	*Tutti*	12-bar blues (B♭ minor)
13–28	Sax	**16 bars** (B♭ major)
29–52	Trumpet	12-bar blues (B♭ major)
		12-bar blues (B♭ major)
53–64	Piano	12-bar blues (B♭ major)
65–76	Trombone	12-bar blues (B♭ major)
77–86	Trumpet	12-bar blues (B♭ major), interrupted after the first seven bars by a modulation to ...
87–90	*Tutti*	Coda (B♭ minor)

➤ The first blues chorus is an adaptation of a popular ballad that was familiar to both black and white audiences of the day, and the last chorus is interrupted by a coda that offers a pessimistic final comment by quoting from Chopin's Funeral March.

The last of these two quotations is as familiar to audiences today as it was in Ellington's time, but the first requires explanation. The opening 12 bars of NAM 49 are an adaptation of the chorus of *The Holy City*, an immensely popular song by the English composer Stephen Adams. Ellington's lead trumpeter, Bubber Miley, recalled it as a 'spiritual' sung by his mother – which in a sense it was, because black Americans identified with the song's dream of a new Jerusalem, where there would be no more oppression. The following example shows the relationship between the two melodies:

> The music known as Chopin's 'funeral march' is actually an excerpt from the third movement of his second piano sonata.

The last three bars of Adams' tune (not shown *above*) are more freely adapted but remain recognisable in outline. To expand the eight-bar melody to a 12-bar blues structure, the first four bars are spread over eight bars, but Adams' simple harmony needs few changes except – significantly – it has been darkened by being played in the minor mode in *Black and Tan*. Perhaps this is a bleak realisation that the new Jerusalem is just a mirage? As a result of this transformation, the bright major 3rd of B♭ major (D) becomes a much more blues-like minor 3rd (D♭). Its 'blue' quality is heightened with **pitch bends** in bars 3 and 7, and in both cases the D♭ falls to B♭, producing the falling minor 3rd that is one of the most characteristic features of a blues melody.

Ellington uses one of the common structures in jazz, known as a **head arrangement**. This is based on a theme and/or chord progression called the head because it is provides the pattern of chords (known as the **changes**) that the players must keep in their heads and use as the basis for their improvisations. The changes are then repeated by the rhythm section, while a series of soloists improvise new melodies to fit the harmonies. Each repeat of the changes is known as a **chorus**. At the end of the piece there is a section for everyone (**tutti**) which is usually a repeat of the opening theme or a **coda**.

In NAM 49 Ellington adopts the most common of all changes, the 12-bar blues, and he uses the type of head arrangement we have described. The head and the 16-bar section that follows it, together with the coda described *above*, are all composed. Between these sections, bars 29–84 are improvised. The trombonist makes some occasional references to the composed theme heard in the head, such as the fall from tonic to dominant in bar 65, and the cadential pattern in bar 75, but Duke Ellington seems more attracted to a free-ranging, chromatic style in his own piano solo.

The arrangement

The head (tutti)
Bars 1–12

The Bubber Miley's muted trumpet melody is accompanied mainly in parallel 6ths by clarinet and muted trombone, while the rhythm section provides four accented beats a bar, sometimes in-filled by the piano at the ends of phrases.

The bass outlines the root and 5th of each chord in steady crotchets. The head is **diatonic** (apart from a passing D♮) and its minor-key mood is severe, with narrow instrumental ranges, mournful **pitch bends** and no display of virtuosity.

16-bar alto sax solo
Bars 13–28

A complete change of mood occurs with a transition to the major mode, together with 'western' chromatic harmonies that complement the 'western' 16-bar structure, and the mellifluous tone of the saxophone. The wide **vibrato** and almost constant use of **portamento** (gliding between notes) in this solo are characteristic of saxophone playing in the early 20th century.

> In jazz, a chord that replaces one with a similar harmonic function is known as a **substitution chord**. For example, a jazz musician might decide to play vii$^{\text{dim.7}}$ instead of V^7 as the first chord of a perfect cadence.

The difference in harmonic style is just as significant, including a chromatic **substitution chord** (G♭^{7} instead of F^7 in bars 13–14 and 21–22) and a rapid **cycle of 5ths** in bars 19–20. The solo is also rhythmically more complex than the head, particularly in its use of cross-phrasing (the patterns of three quavers that cross the usual divisions of beats and bar-lines in bars 17–18 and 25–26). The first eight bars of this section are given a varied repeat in bars 21–28, still with an accompaniment of chords on low reeds. Quickly choked (damped) cymbal notes in bar 28 signal the end of what we might term the 'tan' section, ready for a return to the 'black' sound of the blues changes that is about to occur in bar 29.

The style of writing in the first two sections of this piece would probably have required notated parts rather than improvisation. But from bar 29 until bar 84 Ellington makes provision for a series of improvised solos that each act as a showcase for the talents of his principal players.

Double chorus: trumpet solo
Bars 29–52

> A plunger mute looks like the rubber suction cup at the end of a plumber's plunger. It results in a very thin tone when held directly in front of the bell of a brass instrument.

At bar 29 the blues progression returns and Ellington's co-writer, lead trumpeter Bubber Miley, takes two consecutive choruses (a total of 24 bars). Virtuosity immediately comes to the fore with his slide up to a top B♭, held for four bars. Much of the rest of the solo features Miley's rhythmic freedom as an improviser, which is thrown into relief by the stark accompaniment from the rhythm section. His melodic style is characterised by frequent **blue notes** (the flattened 3rd and 7th of B♭ major – D♭ and A♭ respectively) and slides, as well as by his use of a plunger mute and the growling effects that are such a feature of Ellington's jungle style.

The growl (also used later in the trombone solo) involved using a small straight mute inserted into the bell of the instrument. The sound was then produced by shaping the mouth cavity to amplify a gargling from the throat while producing the required pitch with the lips and valves in the usual way. A plunger mute was also used to modify the sound. It can be held close to the bell to suppress the sound, as in bars 29–32, or moved further away for a more open sound, as in bar 33. Listen carefully for the frequent transitions between different positions of the mute. In jazz, pairs of quavers are normally **swung** (in other words, played unevenly so that the first quaver of a pair is a little longer than the second). The reference to 'straight quavers' in bar 45 means that these notes are not swung, but are instead played evenly.

The backing remains mainly simple and triadic, harmonic interest arising from the interaction of the improvisation against the chords of the 12-bar blues. However, 7ths are sometimes added (bars 32 and 33) and chord substitutions start to appear – for instance, ii^7 (Cm^7) instead of V in bars 37 and 49.

Piano solo
Bars 52–64

Ellington enters during the last note of the trumpet solo in bar 52, starting his piano solo with a long **anacrusis** (know as a 'pick-up' in jazz) to avoid losing momentum. This section forms a **break** (an unaccompanied solo) and the absence of other instruments allows Ellington much greater freedom with the blues harmony. Chord subsitutions can thus become much more adventurous, including:

➢ Secondary dominant chords (C^7–F^7–B♭^{7} in bars 54–55, leading to E♭ in bar 56 and thus forming part of a **circle of 5ths**)

➢ A **diminished-7th** chord in bar 58 (beats 2–4)

➢ A longer circle-of-5ths progression in bars 59^3–63.

Duke Ellington plays in a style known as stride bass because of the wide leaps in the left hand (seen also in NAM 48, page 463). Ellington's right hand is equally athletic, with more wide leaps and rapid decoration (e.g. bar 61). Between them, both hands cover a very wide range of the keyboard.

Trombone solo
Bars 65–76

The rhythm section and jungle style return for Joe Nanton's solo (the band nicknamed him 'Tricky Sam' because of his dexterity in juggling the trombone slide and plunger mute in the same hand). Like Bubber Miley he uses two mutes, a small trumpet mute placed in the bell of the trombone and a plunger mute held in the hand. He plays in the trombone's highest range and, with the plunger held close to the bell, produces an almost trumpet-like tone at the start. The plunger is moved away from the bell for the growl in bar 67, and this is followed by the characterstic 'wah-wah' sound as the mute is then moved in front of the bell and away again.

One of Nanton's most famous effects occurs in bars 72–73. Known popularly as a 'horse whinny', it begins with an upward **glissando** produced by increasing lip pressure without moving the slide. It is followed by a long downward glissando produced by jagged movements of the slide to introduce ripples as the pitch descends.

Trumpet solo and coda
Bars 76–90

In many head arrangements, each successive soloist seems to try to outdo the previous one in virtuoso technique. In this, his second solo, Miley focuses on fast lip trills and the brilliant articulation of rapidly repeated pitches. However, this chorus is brought to a premature end by the unexpected entry of the reeds in bar 84. A series of secondary dominants (G$^{7(♭9)}$, C^7 and F^7) leads to a return of B♭ minor and the quotation from Chopin's Funeral March in the last four bars. The gloom of this unhappy little coda is enhanced by a type of ending rarely heard in jazz – a massive *rallentando* over repeated plagal cadences.

Exercise 6

1. Name three features of Ellington's 'jungle style'.

2. What is meant by the term 'the changes' in jazz? What forms the changes in this work?

3. The first chorus (or head) is played *tutti*. What does *tutti* mean?

4. Compare the melodic ranges used in the first chorus and coda with the melodic ranges used in the other choruses.

5. Explain the terms 'subsitution chord' and 'pick-up'.

6. What is the meaning of 'straight ♪s' in bar 45?

7. Give one example of each of the following types of blue note in bars 29–52: (i) a flat 3rd, (ii) a flat 5th, and (iii) a flat 7th.

8. Where is there a segment of a circle of 5ths *after* bar 64?

9. Comment on the role played by the rhythm section in NAM 49.

Quartet Op. 22: movement 1 (Webern)

Style

One of the features of late 19th-century music was a tendency to fire up the emotional tension by using successions of chromatic dissonances over complex chords that seldom resolve on tonic harmony.

| NAM 8 (page 160)   CD1 Track 10 |
| Jacqueline Ross (violin) |
| Ruth MacDowell (clarinet) |
| Jan Steele (saxophone) |
| Mark Racz (piano) |

Some early 20th-century composers, such as Arnold Schoenberg, continued to develop this trend, their dissonances becoming longer and their resolutions ever briefer, until familiar signposts such as tonic and dominant chords became rare. By 1908 Schoenberg realised that by abandoning the concept of key entirely he could use expressive dissonance as freely as he wanted.

However, without key centres to act as focal points this **atonal** music at first proved difficult to structure and it was sometimes hard to prevent one particular note sounding like a home note. To help avoid this problem Schoenberg adopted (in the early 1920s) a technique known as **serialism**, in which a series of notes replaces tonality as the binding agent in the music.

Serial music

The basis of serialism is the arrangement of the 12 pitches of the chromatic scale into a particular series called a **tone row**. Each note can appear only once in the row, thus helping to avoid the sense that any individual pitch is more important than the others. The row can be used forwards (called the **prime order**), backwards (known as **retrograde**), in melodic **inversion** or both backwards an in inversion (**retrograde inversion**). It can be transposed and in addition any note may be used in any octave. However in strict 12-tone music the pitches must always appear in one of these predetermined patterns – and that is what gives such 12-tone (or dodecaphonic) music its sense of unity and order.

Although the concepts behind serialism may sound mathematical, they produced some highly concentrated, expressive, but very dissonant music. The technique was used by Schoenberg's pupils, Berg and Webern, and by other 20th-century composers, such as Stravinsky (in the later part of his life), Boulez and Stockhausen.

Webern was also interested in contrapuntal techniques, especially in the music of Bach, and in his mature works he avoided anything that hints at Romanticism, so do not expect to find sequences, familiar chords or lyrical melodies – his preference was for angular leaps of 7ths and 9ths. Webern's compositions are highly condensed and very short, and often written for unusual combinations of instruments, as in this quartet.

Context and forces

Schoenberg, Berg and Webern all lived in Vienna and are collectively known as the Second Viennese School. The First Viennese School includes Haydn, Mozart and Beethoven, who all worked in and around Vienna in the Classical period. The word 'school' in this context refers to similarities in style and not to any sort of educational establishment!

In 1928 Webern announced to his publisher that he was planning 'a new work: a concerto for violin, clarinet, horn, piano, and string orchestra, in the spirit of some of Bach's *Brandenburg* concertos', which he planned to be in three movements. However, by the time he had finished the work in 1930, it had shrunk to a two-movement quartet for the highly unusual combination of violin, clarinet, saxophone and piano – four highly contrasting timbres.

The instrumental writing is demanding, although not overly difficult (the pianist, for instance, rarely has to play more than one note at a time in each hand). Nevertheless, the work is most likely to be played by professional musicians at specialist concerts of modern music.

The clarinet and saxophone are transposing instruments, but their parts are printed at sounding pitch in NAM, making it easier to read this complex score. Notice that almost every note is marked with some kind of instruction. Terms in German can be looked up on page 537 of NAM.

Structure

It takes time to get to grips with Webern's sound-world, but when you listen to the movement can you identify its overall shape? The music doesn't really seem to get going until bar 6, as if the first five bars are just an introduction, and the middle section (bars 16–23) seems to be differentiated by more activity, louder dynamics and wider leaps. At the end of bar 22 the five octaves between the high C on the violin and the low C in the left hand of the piano forms the widest range of notes anywhere in the piece – it is clearly a central climax. If you compare bar 28 with bar 6 you might spot that there are similarities – in fact the final part is a varied repeat of bars 6–15.

This gives us the structure shown *right* – an introduction followed by what is essentially a **ternary form** (ABA). The three sections marked * all use related material. In fact a more precise (if rather less obvious) description of the structure would be a modernised version of **sonata form**. The main parts of this are labelled in the diagram *right*: the principal ideas are presented in an exposition, they are manipulated in various ways in a development, and then they return in altered form in a recapitulation. This is a structure found in such Classical pieces as Beethoven's Septet, although in that style sonata form is based on the relationship between different keys which is clearly not the case here.

Bars		Structure
1–5		* Introduction
6–15	A	Exposition
16–23	B	Development
24–27		* Link
28–39	A	Recapitulation
39–43		* Coda

Rhythm

J. S. Bach had a fascination with the study of numerology – the meaning of numbers – and it is clear that he was aware that if the alphabet is translated into numbers (a=1, b=2, and so on) the name Bach can be represented by 14 (2+1+3+8) – a number that he often incorporated into his music in various ways. 'J. S. Bach' adds up to 41, the reverse of the digits 14 (I and J being the same in the Latin alphabet with which he was familiar). This interest in numbers was shared by Webern, so it seems unlikely that the 41-bar length of the movement was mere coincidence.

Can you spot that almost every rhythm in NAM 8 is derived from the three patterns shown *left*?

The first of these rhythmic cells is played in bar 1 by the saxophone, and is immediately repeated by the violin in bar 2. The second is introduced by the left hand of the piano in bar 3 and is immediately repeated in the right hand. The third starts at the end of bar 3 in the violin and is immediately repeated by the saxophone and then the clarinet.

While the rhythms themselves sound very modern the technique of basing a piece on a small number of repeated rhythms is very common in the music of J. S. Bach and many other Baroque composers. Another more subtle reference to Bach comes in the length of the piece. NAM 8 appears to show 43 bar numbers, but Webern himself numbered the second-time bars on the last page as variants of the first-time bars, giving 41 bars in all. The significance of this, and the potential homage it pays to the name of J. S. Bach is shown in the margin note, *left*.

The note row

The basic series of 12 pitches (called the prime order) on which this movement is based is most easily seen in the saxophone part of bars 6–10. Since this is the untransposed form of the prime order, we call it P^0:

P^0 ▶	C♯	E	F	D	D♯	B	B♭	A	G♯	F♯	C	G	

This entire row can be transposed to any of the other 11 pitches in an octave, and we can use superscript numerals to indicate the amount of upward transposition. P^1 is a semitone higher than P^0, P^2 is two semitones higher than P^0, and so on:

P^0 ▶	C♯	E	F	D	D♯	B	B♭	A	G♯	F♯	C	G	◀ R^0
P^1 ▶	D	F	F♯	D♯	E	C	B	B♭	A	G	C♯	G♯	◀ R^1
P^2 ▶	D♯	F♯	G	E	F	C♯	C	B	B♭	G♯	D	A	◀ R^2

The retrograde versions of these transpositions (R^0, R^1, R^2 and so on) can be seen by reading these rows from right to left.

We can use this technique to construct a matrix (known as a 'magic square') of all the possible permutations of the row. This is shown at the top of the next page. The prime orders of the row are read from left to right, retrograde versions from right to left. Inversions of the row are read from top to bottom of a column, and retrograde inversions are read from bottom to top of a column.

The permutations actually used by Webern in this movement (15 out of a possible 48) are labelled in bold type. When following these remember that notes may be printed enharmonically in the score (e.g. E♭ for D♯) and that they may appear in any octave.

Also, be aware that notes of the series may occur simultaneously in the piano (e.g. in bar 12, notes 2 and 3 of I^0 appear as a chord in the right hand and are immediately mirrored by notes 2 and 3 of P^{10} in the left hand). This is a process in serial music known as **verticalisation** of the row.

	I⁰ ▼	I³	I⁴	I¹	I²	I¹⁰ ▼	I⁹ ▼	I⁸	I⁷	I⁵	I¹¹ ▼	I⁶ ▼	
P⁰ ▶	C#	E	F	D	D#	B	Bb	A	G#	F#	C	G	
P⁹	Bb	C#	D	B	C	G#	G	F#	F	D#	A	E	
P⁸	A	C	C#	Bb	B	G	F#	F	E	D	G#	D#	
P¹¹ ▶	C	D#	E	C#	D	Bb	A	G#	G	F	B	F#	◀ R¹¹
P¹⁰ ▶	B	D	D#	C	C#	A	G#	G	F#	E	Bb	F	◀ R¹⁰
P²	D#	F#	G	E	F	C#	C	B	Bb	G#	D	A	
P³	E	G	G#	F	F#	D	C#	C	B	A	D#	Bb	
P⁴ ▶	F	G#	A	F#	G	D#	D	C#	C	Bb	E	B	
P⁵	F#	A	Bb	G	G#	E	D#	D	C#	B	F	C	
P⁷	G#	B	C	A	Bb	F#	F	E	D#	C#	G	D	
P¹ ▶	D	F	F#	D#	E	C	B	Bb	A	G	C#	G#	
P⁶ ▶	G	Bb	B	G#	A	F	E	D#	D	C	F#	C#	
	▲ RI⁰										▲ RI¹¹		

> Many analyses of this work identify the prime as the row we describe as **I⁵**. This is because Webern wrote the second movement of the quartet first, basing it on that version of the row. Since you are studying only the first movement (which never uses **I⁵**) it is more logical to regard the prime as the first 12 notes played by the saxophone in the exposition.

Introduction (bars 1–5)

Commentary

Webern introduces **I⁰** and **P¹⁰** virtually simultaneously, dividing the notes between instruments as shown *below*. For clarity some notes are transposed to a different octave, and remember that notes are often written enharmonically in serial music (so the first saxophone note is Db in the score, but C♯ in the table *above*):

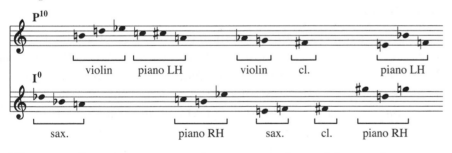

There are three important points to note about this opening:

> ➤ A melody that passes from one instrument to another every few notes is known as **klangfarbenmelodie** (German for 'tone-colour melody'). The technique can also be described as **pointillist** (a term borrowed from painting, where it refers to a texture made from individual dots of colour)

> ➤ Each melodic fragment is imitated in **mirror canon** – for example, the saxophone part in bars 1–2 begins by falling a minor 3rd and then falls by a minor 9th, and this is imitated in inversion (i.e. mirrored) by the violin part in bar 2, which *rises* a minor 3rd and then *rises* by a minor 9th

> ➤ **I⁰** and **P¹⁰** come together in close proximity on F♯ (the two clarinet notes in bar 4 of the score) – Webern almost seems to be defying the principle that all pitches are equal in serial music by giving this note special focus.

Exposition (bars 6–15)

The saxophone announces complete statements of P^0 and P^6, around which the other instruments first play I^6 and P^4 in mirror canon (the second part following the first at a distance of only a semiquaver), and then I^0 and P^{10}, also in mirror canon. Because the unchanging colour of the saxophone melody runs through the whole section, it is sometimes described as a **cantus firmus**. These two different ideas (the cantus firmus and the mirror canons) could be regarded as the first and second subjects of a sonata-form exposition, although they defy convention by occuring simultaneously. Webern does, though, place repeat signs around these ten bars, just like a traditional sonata-form exposition.

Development (bars 16–27)

This falls into four units:

> Bars 16–18 contain mirror canons (I^9 and P^1) in which the two parts are spaced further apart than in the exposition

> Bars 19–21 contain further mirror canons (this time P^0 and I^{10}) that sound almost like a sequence of the previous three bars

> Bars 21–24 contains five simultaneous parts and two mirror canons (using all four forms of transposition 11: R^{11} and RI^{11}, plus I^{11} and P^{11}) – this intense activity, along with the extremes of pitch and the $f\!f$ markings, indicates the climax of the movement at the end of bar 22

> Bars 24–27 form a link to the recapitulation and are based on a modified retrograde version of the introduction, using RI^0 and R^{10} in mirror canon.

Recapitulation (bars 28–39)

The cantus firmus from the exposition returns, now shared between violin, clarinet and saxophone (but still using P^0 and P^6) while the mirror canons are now in the piano (again using the same rows as before). Octave displacement means that intervals are now inverted. For example, in bar 6 the saxophone rose from C♯ to the E above, while in bar 28 the clarinet falls from C♯ to the E below. Webern uses repeat signs to indicate that the whole of the development and recapitulation should be repeated, following a practice that was common in the early history of sonata form.

Coda (bars 39–43)

The material from the introduction is repeated in retrograde form, starting with F–B♭–E in the violin part (which is the retrograde of the left-hand piano part in bar 5). The repeated staccato F♯s (the second of which is notated as G♭) occur in the piano part at the start of bar 40.

Other points

The texture of the whole movement is contrapuntal but very sparse – tiny groups of notes are separated by many rests in this pointillist style. This also means that while most bars are in $\frac{3}{8}$ time, there is no obvious sense of pulse or metre, especially as many of the motifs begin on weak parts of the bar. The harmony is dissonant and there is no sense of tonality as the music is entirely atonal.

At the end of bar 22 the most extreme range of the piece occurs between the high C in the violin and the low C in the piano. These notes are each exactly two and a half octaves away from the clarinet's F♯ in bar 4. This F♯ acts as a sort of central axis for the movement. Notice how all four entries in bar 21 begin on this same F♯.

Note that in some editions of this quartet there is a missing treble clef sign before the last two saxophone notes in bar 42.

Exercise 7

1. What is meant by the terms (a) atonality and (b) mirror canon?

2. Explain what is meant by a tone row and describe the main ways in which it can be transformed in serial music.

3. How does Webern achieve rhythmic unity in this movement?

4. Give the meaning of *mit Dämpfer* in bar 1 and *Dämpfer auf* in bar 24 (both in the violin part).

5. What is a *Klangfarbenmelodie*?

6. What is the texture of this music and in what context would you most likely hear it performed?

7. What do you notice about the dynamics in this movement?

Sample questions

In Section C of the Unit 6 paper you will have to answer one of two questions about the instrumental works you have studied. Your response is expected to be an essay, written in continuous prose, and your clarity of expression, spelling and grammar will be taken into account in the marking.

Remember that it is important to give locations of each specific feature that you mention, but there should not normally be any need to write out music examples. You will be allowed to refer to an unmarked copy of NAM as you write.

Here are two essay topics to use for practice. Aim to complete each essay in 50 minutes.

(a) Compare and contrast approaches to structure and harmony in the three following works:

- Beethoven's Septet in E♭, Op. 20: movement I (NAM 17, pages 207–230)
- Sweelinck's *Pavana Lachrimae* (NAM 20, pages 245–249)
- Debussy's *Pour le piano*: Sarabande (NAM 24, pages 260–261)

(b) Comment on the use of instruments in the three following works:

- Bach's Brandenburg Concerto No. 4 in G: movement I (NAM 1, pages 7–30)
- Webern's Quartet Op. 22: movement I (NAM 8, pages 160–162)
- Ellington and Miley's *Black and Tan Fantasy* (NAM 49, pages 465–468).

Applied music

Prelude to *Tristan und Isolde* (Wagner)

Context

An important aspect of 19th-century Romanticism was a desire to bring the arts together. This is seen particularly in the operas of Richard Wagner, who developed what he called the *Gesamtkunst-werk* (total artwork) for which he alone was responsible for almost every element. To achieve this Wagner wrote his own words, set them to music in a symphonic style for a very large orchestra, supervised every aspect of the production and even designed his own opera house in Bavaria, which was (and still is) dedicated solely to the staging of his music dramas.

NAM 4 is the prelude (or overture) to *Tristan and Isolde*, one of these 'total artworks'. The opera is based on a story about a medieval knight called Tristan who is sent to bring Isolde from Ireland to Cornwall where King Mark is waiting to marry her. But Tristan and Isolde fall in love and betray King Mark's trust with disastrous consequences for them both. The prelude flows straight into the first scene of the opera (the curtain begins to rise in bar 106). This explains why it begins in A minor, but ends with an imperfect cadence in C minor (the opening key of Act One).

Wagner wrote the opera between 1857 and 1859, at a time when he was having an extra-marital affair; its tale of insatiable longing and doomed love probably had personal significance for the composer. Just the prelude was first performed in a concert in 1859, but the opera itself was at first considered unperformable due to its length and difficulty. It was eventually staged for the first time in Munich in 1865, to mainly hostile reviews.

The score

The opera requires a large orchestra of triple woodwind (three of each type of woodwind instrument), with substantial brass and string sections, plus timpani, triangle, cymbals and harp (the last three do not play in the prelude). Wagner also requires a number of instruments to play on stage during the course of the opera.

When reading the score, remember that:

➢ The cor anglais sounds a perfect 5th lower than printed

➢ Clarinets in A, and the bass clarinet, sound a minor 3rd lower than printed

➢ Horns F sound a perfect 5th lower than printed

➢ Horns in E sound a minor 6th lower than printed

➢ Trumpets in F sound a perfect 4th higher than printed

➢ Double basses sound an octave lower than printed.

Note that the C clef (𝄡), which indicates the position of middle C, is used for the viola part and sometimes for other instruments. The direction 'sul G' (e.g. bar 23) is an instruction for the violinists to play on their lowest string, which gives a particularly warm sound. Drum rolls are indicated in the timpani part by the sign *tr* followed by a wavy line.

NAM 4 (page 65)   CD1 Track 4
Vienna Philharmonic Orchestra
Conducted by Georg Solti

One of the most famous aspects of this work is a deliberate tonal ambiguity that arises from lingering on sustained and sometimes unresolved dissonances. The first chord heard in the prelude is so closely associated with the entire opera that it has become known as the 'Tristan chord' (see *right*). In bar 3 this chord is followed by V^7 of A minor (A and A♯ are passing notes), but instead of being followed by chord I there is just a long silence.

These bars are then transposed to end on V^7 of C major in bar 7 but again there is no resolution – only a silence. Another transposition leaves the music poised on an unresolved V^7 of E major in bar 11. This progression is repeated an octave higher in bars 12–13, and then just its last two notes are repeated in bars 14 and 15. In bars 16–17 the melody chromatically surges to a climax – but instead of the long-awaited perfect cadence in A minor, there is an interrupted cadence (V^7–VI) with a long and highly dissonant **appoggiatura** on B above a chord of F major (see *right*).

This process of hinting at a tonic, rather than defining it through functional cadences, is one of the ways in which this work differs from the movements we have studied by Bach and Beethoven. The two earlier composers used tonality to define form, whereas Wagner used it as an expressive agent to foreshadow the longing of the doomed lovers in the opera that begins with this prelude.

Similar procedures can be found throughout the prelude and, along with the frequent use of chromatic dissonances (such as the A♯ in the first music example *above*) help give the music its restless, yearning quality.

Equally distinctive are the long stretches of what Wagner called 'unending melody' – the phrases that join and overlap to give a seamless flow of romantic sound. These melodies are often built up from smaller units called **leitmotifs** (leading motifs). These are another fingerprint of Wagner's style. Each strongly characterised fragment is associated with a particular person, place, object or emotional state in the opera. Just four of these are shown *right*. 'Grief' and 'Desire' are self-explanatory, 'Glance' signifies the moment when Isolde was won over when Tristan looked into her eyes, and 'Love potion' represents the drink that seals their relentless love.

Look at the cello melody in bars 17–22 which is based on motif *x* shown in the music *right* (the 'Glance' motif). This leitmotif itself breaks down into two shorter motifs, *a* and *b*. When *x* begins to repeat in sequence motif *b* is changed from a falling 7th to a falling tone. In bars 19–20 the first note of *x* is tied over while the falling 7th of motif *b* is inverted to a rising 7th.

What makes Wagner's system so complex is the way his 'unending melody' mutates with the ease of microbes. So the 'Love potion' motif (see *right*) is in fact made up of the same two motifs as the 'Glance' motif, but in reverse order and followed by motif *y* from the 'Desire' motif.

The score looks formidable but if you listen for these leitmotifs you will also hear that many parts in the orchestra double each other and that there are rarely more than two principal melodic lines sounding at once.

Tristan chord

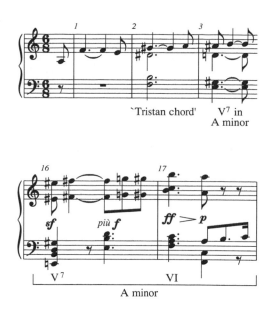

'Tristan chord' V^7 in A minor

V^7 VI

A minor

Unending melody

Grief   cellos

Desire   oboe

Glance   cellos   *a*   *b*   *a*

b   *a*   *b*   *a*   *b*

Love potion   cellos   *b*   *a*

y   *b*   *a*   *y*

Structure and tonality

Bars	
0–24	Exposition
24–65	Middle section
66–83	First recapitulation
82–111	Second recapitulation

Note that the second violins play C♯ on the dotted quaver in bar 24. The sharp sign is missing in some copies of NAM.

When reading the following account, remember that Wagner's 'themes' consist of a number of motifs from later in the opera, as described in the previous section.

Exposition (bars 0–24): A minor/major

Theme 1 (bars 0–17) begins and ends in A minor, concluding with a massive interrupted cadence. It is fragmented into five phrases by lengthy silences (which are omitted in later recapitulations).

Theme 2 (bars 17^4–24, cellos then violins) starts in A minor and then modulates rapidly through D minor and B major to reach the first perfect cadence in the tonic (A major) in bar 24.

Middle section (bars 24^6–65): shifting tonality centred on A
This section forms a **ternary** structure (ABA^1).

Section A begins with **Theme 3** – the eight-bar cello melody in bars 24^6–32^4. It starts in E major, ends on the tonic note (A) without a cadence and is made out of motifs from theme 2, played in reverse order. Section A ends with a repeat of bars 17^4–21 (the beginning of theme 2, now on wind).

Section B (bars 36^4–44) starts with antiphonal development of a motif from theme 2 and ends on a chord of A major.

Section A^1 (bars 45–65) is a reworking of section A and is linked to the next section by a dominant pedal on E (bars 63–70).

First recapitulation (bars 66–83):
A minor/major modulating to V of E♭ minor

Two statements (by oboes and cor anglais) of the 'Desire' motif (first heard in bars 2–3) initiate a compressed recapitulation of the exposition in which rests are omitted and some motifs are condensed (e.g. woodwind, bars 68–74). Meanwhile the strings continue to develop the motif first heard in bars 17^4–18^3 until, at bar 74, they repeat the first four bars of theme 2.

The last part of this section modulates to E♭ minor (the most distant key possible from A minor) for the main climax of the entire prelude. In bars 81–83 Wagner contrapuntally combines all three of his themes over harmony which swings between II^7 (an enharmonic respelling of the 'Tristan chord') and V^7 of E♭ minor in each bar (see *left*). Rapid ascending scales (violins), **tremolo** (violas) and timpani rolls all add to the excitement.

If you find the lack of cadences makes it difficult to follow the score, just listen to the music between timings 7:13 and 7:30 on the CD, where you will hear horns and cellos playing the 'Grief' motif three times, trumpets playing the 'Desire' motif twice, and woodwind playing the 'Glance' motif four times.

This huge build up does not, of course, culminate in a tonic chord, but in the colossal scoring in bar 83 of the 'Tristan chord'. This reveals its tonal ambiguity by resolving not to V^7 of E♭ minor in bar 84, but to V^7 of A minor (as it did in bar 3), as shown in the first example *opposite*. This prepares the way for a restatement of the opening few bars in their original key and a second recapitulation of motifs that were heard earlier.

Second recapitulation (bars 82–111):
A minor modulating to C minor

This second restatement of the main motifs begins with the opening motif of the prelude played by brass and low strings in bar 82 (where it overlaps with the climax of the previous section) and is continued by oboes and cor anglais (see *right*). Instead of the long silences heard in the exposition, the phrases are now linked by motifs in the strings.

The interrupted cadence recurs in bars 93⁴–94 and theme 2 begins in the cellos at bar 94⁴, but the end of the phrase is modified to lead to an imperfect cadence in C minor (bars 99–100).

Woodwind start a third recapitulation (bars 100⁶–106³ are a rescored repeat of bars 0–7) but an intermittent dominant pedal on G, played by the timpanist, anchors the tonality to C minor. The final unaccompanied melody for cellos and double basses links the rising minor 6th with which the work began (G–E♭ in bar 107) with the notes of the 'Tristan chord' played melodically. (As shown *right*, D♯ and G♯ are notated as E♭ and A♭.)

'Tristan chord'   A minor: V⁷

Pitches of the 'Tristan chord'

107   E♭   B   F   A♭

Rising minor 6th

Exercise 8

1. What is a cor anglais? What is the *sounding* pitch of the note played by the cor anglais in bar 2?

2. What is an appoggiatura? Which note on the first beat of bar 37 is an appoggiatura?

3. What do you think is meant by the instruction 'a 3' in the flute part at bar 73?

4. How should the violas play the notes with strokes through their stems in bars 77–83?

5. On the first beat of bar 97, how does the *sounding* pitch of the bass clarinet note relate to the *sounding* pitch of the note played by the double basses on this same beat?

6. Explain what is meant by a *leitmotif*.

7. Why doesn't NAM 4 end in the key in which it began (A minor)?

O Wilhelme, pastor bone (Taverner)

In 1525 Cardinal Wolsey, Archbishop of York and Lord Chancellor to King Henry VIII, founded a magnificent new college at Oxford University. It was named Cardinal College (later changed to Christ Church College) and Wolsey appointed John Taverner, the greatest English composer of the early 16th century, as its first Master of the Choristers the following year.

Wolsey decreed that the duties of the college choir should include the daily singing of an antiphon (an unaccompanied setting of a religious text) in honour of the 12th-century Saint William, one of Wolsey's predecessors as Archbishop of York.

Taverner's *O Wilhelme, pastor bone* must have been written for precisely this purpose, probably in about 1528, since it begins with a plea to William of York ('O Wilheme') and its second stanza includes a prayer for Cardinal Thomas our founder ('Thomam Cardinalem Fundatorem' in bars 36–38).

Context

NAM 26 (page 266)   CD3 Track 1
Christ Church Cathedral Choir Oxford
Conducted by Stephen Darlington

The text is in Latin because England was Roman Catholic at this time, and services were in Latin. There is an translation on page 538 of NAM.

The recording on CD3 is by the choir of Christ Church Oxford (now a cathedral as well as a college chapel). They are the successors of the choir for whom Taverner wrote this work nearly five centuries ago. On CD3 only the treble part is sung by boys; the part for means is sung by adult male altos and the part labelled counter-tenor is sung by tenor voices.

O Wilhelme was intended to be sung **a cappella** (unaccompanied) by an all-male choir. Boys would have sung the two highest parts ('mean' refers to low treble voices). In NAM 26 the counter-tenor and tenor parts are written with vocal tenor clefs – the little figure 8 below the clefs indicate that the notes sound an octave lower than printed, so the first counter-tenor note is middle C and the first tenor note is the F below middle C.

NAM 26 is the oldest piece in the anthology and, like other pieces from long ago, the original setting has been lost. NAM 26 has been reconstructed from a later version of the work, made after Wolsey's fall from power, which has totally different words that make no mention of either the Cardinal or Saint William.

A further complication results from the fact that vocal music in the 16th century was not normally written as a full score, like that seen in the anthology. Instead, pieces would normally be collected into a set of part books: one volume with all the treble parts for various works; another with all the alto parts, and so on. Unfortunately no tenor part has survived for even the later version of this work, and so the one printed in the anthology has been reconstructed by a modern scholar, based on a knowledge of the style and the clues provided by the other parts. It is possible to reconstruct the missing tenor part in other ways, one of which can be heard on the anthology recording. Remember, though, that it is the printed version of NAM 26 that you are required to study.

Word setting

Taverner uses a **syllabic** setting of the text until he reaches the last phrase (*aeternae vitae praemium*) where the end of the work is highlighted with a **melisma** in the upper parts. Each phrase of the text has its own melody and texture, sometimes separated from the following phrase by a decisive cadence, although at other times the end of one phrase overlaps with the beginning of the next.

Texture

Taverner often varies the texture by dividing the choir into different groups of parts. In bars 1–7 the words *O Wilhelme, pastor bone* are first sung in two-part **counterpoint** by high voices then in three parts by low voices, the melody of the uppermost part being exactly repeated an octave lower. This effect of one group of performers being answered by a contrasting group is known as **antiphony**. It also enables Taverner to keep in reserve the full impact of his five-part texture until bar 10.

The first three phrases of the text begin with mainly staggered entries of the parts rather than with the voices starting together. These entries are too dissimilar to be described as imitation, but the fact that the syllables of the text often do not coincide between the parts helps us to notice that we are listening to a combination of simultaneous melody lines. This type of contrapuntal texture is often called **polyphony**, particularly when it occurs in Renaissance music for unaccompanied voices.

Taverner later writes parts that do mainly coincide in rhythm. This is known as a **homophonic** texture and it is one in which the words can be more clearly heard than in polyphony. So it is not surprising to see it used when Taverner wants to highlight the importance of Cardinal Wolsey in bars 38–42.

Notice how the treble phrase in bars 33–37 is repeated by the bass in the antiphonal response of the next five bars. This same phrase then returns to the treble in bars 43–47.

Taverner reserves **imitation** for the final section of the antiphon. Starting in bar 56 each voice sings *Aeternae vitae praemium* to a figure that follows a rising interval with a gentle descent. In bar 64 the trebles reach top F as the basses descend to the F three octaves below. It is probably no accident that the full range of the choir is reserved for this climactic vision of eternity.

Tonality

To our ears, *O Wilhelme* might seem to begin and end in F major, with bars 22^4–52 in G minor. However, the treble E in bar 11 does not not rise to F, as you might expect in tonal music. And at the end of the phrase the chord of B♭ major (bar 12^4) is not followed by a chord of F major on the first beat of bar 13, to form a plagal cadence, but by a chord of A minor (decorated with F–E in the treble part). Similarly the phrases that end in bars 15–16 and 19–20 are harmonised by the progression Gm–F, producing very modal-sounding cadences.

The reason is simple. This music pre-dates the tonal system, and is essentially **modal**, even though many of the cadences in the first section end on a chord of F major. Similarly, while the next section might seem like G minor, the lack of printed F♯s before the chord of G in the cadences at bars 31–32 and bar 52 again indicate the essentially modal character of this music.

Harmony

NAM 26 consists entirely of triads in root position (sometimes without a 3rd) and first inversion. There is not a single on-the-beat discord in the antiphon. Instead, Taverner makes use of a particularly English device – a 6th falling to a 5th above a static bass. An expressive example occurs in bar 15 where the treble E♭ (a 6th above the bass G) falls to D to complete a G-minor triad. In the next bar, this D is tied over the barline to form a 6th above F which then falls to C to complete a chord of F-major.

The most startling example of this technique occurs in bar 32 where the 6th–5th above the bass (E–D in the mean) is combined with a **tierce de Picardie** (B♮ in the treble) to form a totally unexpected chord of E minor in first inversion, which becomes a triad of G major when the mean falls from E to D.

The tierce de Picardie is an integral part of the English polyphonic style of this period, as is the **false relation**. A pungent example occurs at the start of bar 41, where the E♭ in the bass part is both preceded and followed by E♮ in the countertenor part.

A tierce de Picardie is a major 3rd in the final tonic chord of a passage in a minor key. Here, the key is G minor, but the tierce de Picardie (B♮) results in a chord of G *major* in bar 32.

A false relation occurs when a note in its normal form and in a chromatic form (such as E and E♭) occur in two different parts at either the same time or in close proximity.

Melody and rhythm

The mean has a compass of an 11th, the bass a 10th and the other three parts encompass only a 9th. Phrase lengths are determined by the text and are not governed by a preference for two, four and eight bar units found in later styles of music – for example, bars 33–47 contain three clearly separated five-bar phrases.

Taverner combines **conjunct** movement with generally small leaps to create phrases that often have an elegant arch shape, as in the opening treble melody. If the leap is wider than a 3rd, he usually prefers to return to a note within the leap, as in bar 2 of the opening treble melody. The mean in bars 22 and 31 is an exception, containing angular lines that are rare in 16th-century polyphony. However, leaps are of necessity more frequent in the bass part because it sometimes consists of roots of chords that are a 5th apart (as in bars 23⁴–27).

Totally stepwise movement is infrequent, but when it does occur it is particularly expressive. In the treble part of bars 13–16, for instance, the conjunct ascent and descent throws the modal flat 7th (E♭) into relief, vividly expressing the word *agone* (strife). Whenever this note occurs it draws attention to the text since the melodic lines basically conform to F major at the beginning and end of the work, and G minor from the last beat of bar 22 to bar 52. Thus, in the treble part of bars 33–37 an almost complete ascending scale and a conjunct descent (both with E♮) is followed by an E♭ on the first syllable of *Thomam Cardinalem*.

Exercise 9

1. Explain the meaning of a cappella singing.

2. How does the vocal tenor clef differ from the treble clef?

3. What type of voice is meant by a 'mean'?

4. Explain what is meant by the following statement:
   Bars 1–10 of NAM 26 consist of antiphonal exchanges.

5. What is the difference between syllabic and melismatic word setting? Give an example of each type from NAM 26.

6. Which two notes form a false relation in bars 28–29?

7. What term describes the texture of bars 48–49?

8. Explain the meaning of a tierce de Picardie and give an example of one in bars 48–56.

Quoniam tu solus from 'The Nelson Mass' (Haydn)

Context

Although the style of this excerpt is totally different to Taverner's *O Wilhelme*, it is another example of Latin church music intended to be sung as part of a service. It comes from a mass, the most important service in the Roman Catholic church. Musical settings of the mass usually have five main sections, each sung at a different point in the service. NAM 29 comes from the second of these sections, called the *Gloria* – a joyful text of praise.

> NAM 29 (page 299)   CD3 Track 7
> Barbara Bonney (soprano)
> London Symphony Chorus
> City of London Sinfonia
> Conducted by Richard Hickox

By the end of the 18th century, settings of the mass for grand occasions often required, as here, orchestral accompaniment and solo voices as well as a choir. The influence of opera is evident in the ornate writing for soloists and the influence of the symphony in the orchestral writing. In fact, Haydn divided the *Gloria* into three sections (Allegro–Adagio–Allegro, of which NAM 29 is the last) like a three-movement symphony or concerto.

This elaborate type of church music was particularly popular in and around Vienna during the Classical period, and has come to be known as the Viennese Classical Mass.

Towards the end of his long life, one of Haydn's few remaining official duties was to write settings of the mass for the name day of Princess Maria, wife of his patron Prince Nikolaus II of Esterháza (one of the chief aristocrats of the Austrian empire).

A name day is the church feast day of the saint after whom somebody is named.

When Haydn wrote this mass in 1798 his original title was *Missa in angustiis* (Mass in time of fear), reflecting the terror of the Napoleonic wars then threatening Europe. That same year Admiral Nelson decimated Napoleon's navy and when in 1800 Nelson visited Austria (and met Haydn) it is likely that this mass was one of the works performed in the admiral's honour. It was certainly at that time that the work acquired the nickname 'Nelson Mass'.

The first performance took place in September 1798, when it formed part of a church service with each of its five movements being separated by readings and prayers. The work is still sometimes performed this way, as part of the communion service on special occasions in Anglican cathedrals and chapels. However, the work is now more likely to be heard as part of a concert in a church or concert hall, in which case each movement follows straight on from the one before.

One of the consequences of the 'time of fear' mentioned in the official title of this work was a political and financial instability that led Prince Esterházy to lay off most of the wind players in his court orchestra shortly before Haydn composed 'The Nelson Mass'. Consequently it was written for a small ensemble of strings, trumpets, timpani and organ (the organist providing some of the solo lines that might otherwise have been given to woodwind).

Instrumentation

The version in NAM 29 has woodwind parts added by a modern editor. However, you do not have to study the orchestration in detail, as the work is presented in vocal score. This shows all of the parts for the singers, but the orchestral parts are condensed onto two staves, suitable for a pianist to play in rehearsals.

If you play through the accompaniment you will find that much of it makes perfectly good musical sense without the vocal parts. This is one of the reasons why the Viennese Classical Mass is often described as symphonic. For much of the movement the chorus either sing a simplified version of the orchestral parts (bars 3–22 and 57–61) or they double the orchestral parts (bars 22–57).

NAM 29 falls into three parts, differentiated by texture:

Structure and texture

➢ Bars 1–22 are **homophonic**

➢ Bars 22–61 are **fugal** and

➢ Bars 62–82 are freely **contrapuntal**.

In addition, the way in which the relatively simple soprano melody is duplicated by a more elaborate version of the same material in the orchestra is known as a **heterophonic** texture. Everything is carried irresistibly forward by this symphonic orchestral writing.

The first two sections of the *Gloria* are not included in NAM 29, but the movement as a whole is in ternary form (ABA[1]). Much of NAM 29 is a varied reprise of music heard in the opening section of the *Gloria*.

Commentary

Section 1 (homophonic)

The movement begins with **antiphonal** exchanges between solo soprano and full choir. Bars 2–9^1 are then repeated in a fully choral version (bars 9–15^1) after which bars 16–22^1 contain a hushed choral setting of the last line of text over a tonic pedal, which at the last moment moves to the dominant (A major).

The harmonies in this first section are mainly diatonic, with much use of chords I and V.

Section 2 (fugal)

The two-bar fugue **subject** starting in bar 22 is sung by the basses and accompanied by a **countersubject** of staccato quavers in the orchestra. Notice the use a short sequence in both parts.

When the tenors enter with a slightly altered version of the subject in bar 24 the basses sing the countersubject. This pattern continues until all the vocal parts have entered. The basses restate the subject in bar 30, then the tenors begin a modulatory passage by singing the subject in the key of B minor.

The terrific sense of excitement in the rest of this section is largely attributable to Haydn's use of **stretto** (a contrapuntal device in which imitative entries are condensed). Thus the sopranos enter in bar 33, just one bar after the tenors – and all three upper parts enter at one-bar intervals in bars 46–48. The fugal texture fizzles out as sopranos and altos descend through a series of suspensions (bars 57–60) to a perfect cadence in the tonic (bars 60–61).

Section 3 (mainly contrapuntal)

The section from bar 62 to the end forms a **coda** to the whole movement. Tonic and dominant harmonies over a tonic pedal support imitative entries from bass, tenor and alto soloists, while the soprano sings a triadic descant. Bars 62–68^1 are repeated to form bars 71–77^1 after which the full choir takes over for the final six bars of the movement.

Exercise 10

1. Which of the five movements in a standard musical setting of the mass is the *Gloria*?

2. Which section of the *Gloria* (first, second or third) is the excerpt in NAM 29?

3. Name the key in bar 4 and state which pitch is purely chromatic decoration in this bar.

4. In bar 9 the choir begins a varied repeat of bars 1–8. How does Haydn achieve a smooth transition from the first eight bars?

5. Compare bars bars 13–14 with bars 7–8.

6. What is the difference between a subject and an answer in a fugue?

7. What is the meaning of stretto?

8. What circumstances prompted Haydn to write sacred music on such a grand scale in this mass?

Titanic (1997): 'Take her to sea, Mr Murdoch' (Horner)

James Horner was born in Los Angeles in 1953. His family moved to London where he attended the Royal College of Music before returning to America to complete his studies. His first film score to achieve great success was *Star Trek II* (1982) and his many subsequent credits include *Aliens* (1986), *Braveheart* (1995), *The Mask of Zorro* (1998) and *All the King's Men* (2006).

Horner's compositional style is conservative and it has been criticised for lack of originality. However, it has proved popular and the huge commercial success of *Titanic* resulted in Horner becoming one of the best known film composers of his generation.

The 1997 film *Titanic* is based on the true and tragic story of the great ocean liner which sank on its maiden voyage in 1912, but it is presented in Hollywood epic style and threaded through with a love story, to give a blockbuster mix of romance and drama. The film also focuses on the ship's Irish passengers sailing to America in the hope of starting a new life. Horner had already shown his interest in Celtic folk music in his score for *Braveheart*, and much of his score for Titanic is based on the styles of, and quotations from, the folk music of Ireland.

NAM 47 accompanies a scene in which Titanic is about to sail out into the open sea and occurs at about 30'30" into the film. The excerpt in NAM is from a concert version of the music. This is mostly similar to the original, although bars 45–63 do not appear in the film.

Much of the excerpt is based on a folksong called 'The Leaving of Liverpool', which has been known since at least the late 19th century. It is not certain if the song originated in Ireland, but it has been recorded by many Irish folk bands. Here is the first line:

Context

NAM 47 (page 440)   CD4 Track 6
City of Prague Philharmonic
Conducted by Nic Raine

See http://youtu.be/EIIVX5NDs4I for a performance of the complete folksong.

The first 29 bars of NAM 46 consists of short passages designed to build-up excitement through the use of:

➤ **Imitation** of a rising figure based on the opening of the melody *above*, transposed to the key of E♭ major (bars 1–3)

➤ A more rhythmic motif which includes semiquavers and that is repeated over a rising bass (bars 4–7)

➤ **Ostinato** patterns over **pedal** notes (bars 8–20)

➤ Rising scale figures (starting at bar 21) which culminate in a climax at bar 28.

➤ A series of modulations that rise in major 3rds from the opening key of E♭ major through G major (bar 8) to B major (bar 15) – movement between keys a 3rd (or 6th) apart is known as a **tertiary shift** and is a well-tried way of creating excitement. (Horner likes it so much that he uses it twice in these opening bars, and again later in the extract.)

Commentary

In bars 1–3 Horner adds a sharpened 4th (A♮) between notes 3 and 4 of 'The Leaving of Liverpool', hinting at the folk-like Lydian mode. The A♭s expected in the key of E♭ major do not appear until bars 6 and 7.

Horner closely matches his music to the visual images of the film. We hear the distant sound of a ship's bell from bar 10. Then, when the camera shows the vast engine room, a very low pedal on D reverberates at the bottom of the orchestra (bars 11–14). As we see shots of the huge boilers being stoked and the propellers spinning faster the tempo progressively increases (bars 19, 23 and 25). The sequences of ascending scales (bar 21 onwards) accompany pictures of mighty pistons at work and close-ups of the pressure gauges rising as the steam power builds up.

Horner settles on the tonal centre of G major for the next choral section (bars 30–36). This purely diatonic music is underpinned by a tonic pedal on G, which briefly gives way for a bass note on the dominant (D) in the second half of bar 33, both features contributing to the strong sense of G-major tonality in this passage.

The change of mood at bar 30 coincides with the film moving to an exterior shot of the Titanic speeding across a calm, sunlit ocean. The heroic choral theme at this point is clearly based on 'The Leaving of Liverpool', although the choir **vocalises** rather than sings the words, and Horner restricts melodic movement to the upper voices. He also makes various small changes to both the rhythm and pitches of the original folksong.

At bar 37 Horner introduces a contrasting idea, although it is based on the melodic shape of the first complete bar of 'The Leaving of Liverpool'. It has something of the character of a folk dance, and first appears in $\frac{5}{4}$ time and G major. It is harmonised mainly with simple root-position triads and there is a folk-like reference to the modal flat seventh (a chord of F major in the key of G) in bars 43–44. The quaver–dotted crotchet pattern (known as a 'Scotch snap') in bars 43 and 44 is another reference to Celtic folk music styles.

This dance idea then alternates with the folksong melody for the rest of the extract, to give the structure shown *left*.

Bars	Section	Key
1–29	Introduction	E♭ → G → B
30–36	'Folksong'	G
37–50	'Dance' in $\frac{5}{4}$	G
51–67	'Folksong'	G → D
68–85	'Dance' in $\frac{6}{4}$	D
86–110	'Folksong'	B

The folksong returns at bar 51, first vocalised by upper voices in G major and then restated by unison violins in a varied version in D major over a tonic pedal on D (bar 57). The note values of the melody in bars 51 and 57 (and at bar 86) are twice the length of those at bar 30. Technically this is an augmentation, but in reality it is simply a by-product of the change to double speed at bar 37.

The dance section returns at bar 68, but now in D major, $\frac{6}{4}$ time and with much more static harmonies heard initially over a tonic pedal (compare this with the frequent changes of chord when this music first appeared in bar 37). In the film, this music accompanies a scene in which the hero (Jack) and his friend hang over the bows of the ship, watching dolphins dart through the waves. The harp **glissando** and suspended cymbal roll in bar 79 are timed to coincide precisely with a dolphin leaping above the bow wave of the ship.

The folksong theme returns again in bar 86, now in B major and scored only for instruments. Notice that Horner again uses the emotional 'lift' of a tertiary shift (from D major to B major), this time to underpin Jack's exhilarating cry of 'I'm the king of the world', which occurs at bar 86 in the film.

Fragments of the folksong theme persist into the final bars. Notice the syncopated **countermelody** for horns and violas that briefly emerges in bar 90, and the rather modal-sounding harmonies of bars 94–97, where root-position triads of G, A and D major impinge on the key of B major, creating in the process a **false relation** between the violins' G♯ on the last beat of bar 95 and the bass G♮ on the very next beat.

Some quiet but dissonant chords, especially in bars 99–100, eventually resolve to a tonic chord of B major that lasts throughout the last five bars of the extract. Above this a solo horn refers back to the version of the opening of the folksong with a Lydian 4th that was heard at the start of the extract, although now in $\frac{2}{2}$ rather than $\frac{3}{4}$ time. The horn is then echoed by a flute, doubled by clarinet and glockenspiel. In the film, this music accompanies a long shot of Titanic steaming away from the camera. The extract ends on a bare-5th chord (B in the strings below F♯ in the woodwind).

> The final bars are in B major, and so the raised (Lydian) 4th is E♯. This is notated as B♯ in the horn part, which sounds a 5th lower than written.

Horner uses the traditional medium of a large orchestra for his score, but the instrumentation is given a more contemporary feel by the addition of 'synth voices' to contrast with the vocalising of the real choir. The orchestration includes considerable **doubling** of parts and a wide range of percussion instruments to help depict the passage of Titanic through the waves. The latter include timpani, suspended cymbal, side drum, bass drum, tam tam (gong), tubular bells, bell tree, sleigh bells and glockenspiel.

> Although much of the score is based on Celtic folk music, Horner doesn't used traditional Irish folk instruments. This is possibly to distinguish his own music from the genuinely Irish folk music played by the group Gaelic Storm, as part of the diegetic music in the film (that is, music which is 'heard' by the characters in the film, rather than background music heard only by people watching the drama).

Exercise 11

1. Name the folksong on which Horner based much of the music in this extract.

2. How does vocalising differ from normal singing?

3. What is a tertiary shift?

4. Explain what is meant by the term doubling when referring to orchestral writing.

5. Which part has two 'Scotch snap' rhythms in bar 75?

6. Which note of the major scale is raised by a semitone to form the Lydian mode?

7. What is special about the final chord in this extract?

Yellow Bird (traditional)

The origin of many of the pieces in the world music section of NAM is obscure, and this is particularly true of *Yellow Bird*. In 1883 Oswald Durand, a famous poet from the Caribbean country of Haiti, published a poem called *Choucoune*, which was set to music ten years later by Michel Mauleart Monton, an American-Haitian composer. This setting is the music we now know as *Yellow Bird*. Some of the material he used in the piece was assembled from existing works (a common practice in popular music of the time) that may possibly have come originally from France – the country that had settled Haiti before it gained independence.

Context

> NAM 60 (page 528)   CD4 Track 18
> Red Stripe Ebony Steelband

A recording of *Choucoune* can be heard at http://youtu.be/kgqq0Upqkx8 – the similarity with *Yellow Bird* is obvious in the chorus, which starts at 00'52".

Calypsos were traditionally sung at carnival time in Port of Spain, the capital of Trinidad. The repertoire was based on about 50 tunes to which new words were constantly improvised – sometimes mocking and satirical, and often topical.

In the first half of the 20th century, *Choucoune* (by then usually known as *Ti Zwaso* or 'Little Bird') was usually performed as a type of dance music known as méringue, which in Haiti was usually quite slow and sentimental. The song was not widely known outside of Haiti until 1957, when the American singer Harry Belafonte released an English version of *Choucoune* under the title 'Don't Ever Love Me'.

That same year, a new version of the song appeared under the title 'Yellow Bird'. It was given totally new words that refer to an unfaithful wife or girlfriend, and that begin:

> Yellow bird, up high in banana tree.
> Yellow bird, you sit all alone like me.
> Did your lady friend leave the nest again?
> That is very bad, makes me feel so sad.
> You can fly away, in the sky away
> You more lucky than me.

The music was arranged in *calypso* style by the American Norman Luboff. This is the version that has been recorded many times over the years and is now so well known that it is often assumed to be a traditional *calypso* from Trinidad. It is also sometimes said to be an example of *mento* from Jamaica – a folk style that predates *ska* and *reggae*, and that is similar to *calypso*.

Perhaps the most accurate way to describe *Yellow Bird* is modern folk music which, while it once had a named composer, originated in some distant age and has continued to evolve ever since.

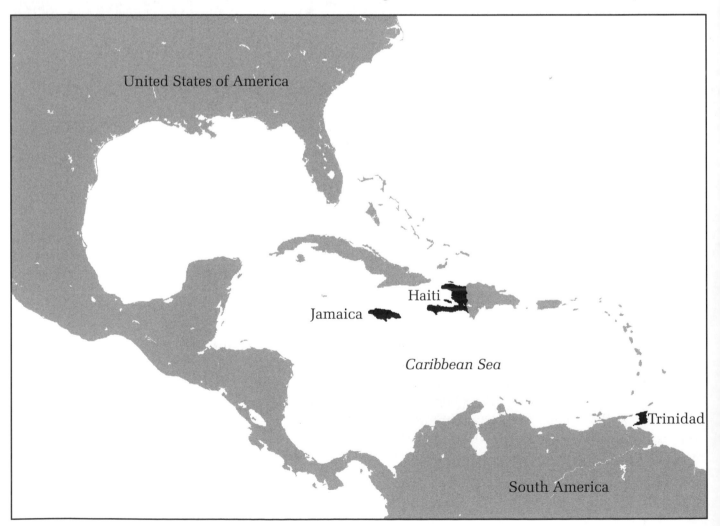

Most calypsos are in a major key, with simple triadic melodies that can be harmonised with the common chords I, IV and V. They are usually in duple metre (*Yellow Bird* is effectively in $\frac{2}{2}$ despite its $\frac{4}{4}$ time signature) and the rhythm often includes **syncopation**. All of these features can be heard in NAM 60. Listen to the whole piece and answer the following questions:

1. How many *different* chords are used in the piece?
2. What instrument do you hear that is not in the score?
3. How are the long notes sustained by the melody instruments?

The rhythm of this arrangement derives from the samba, a Latin-American dance from nearby South America. Notice that while the melody is syncopated, the bass forms a simple rhythmic **ostinato** in which the note values (♩. ♪♪ ♩) are the same in every bar.

However, the structure of *Yellow Bird* is distinctly European with its succession of mainly four-bar phrases falling into verse-and-chorus form. Equally western is the harmony – you probably noticed that it is all based on the primary triads (I, IV and V) sometimes enlived with 7ths and a little chromatic decoration. But the instrumentation sounds characteristically Trinidadian, even though steel pans have spread from Trinidad to other Caribbean countries, as well as to other parts of the world such as Britain.

Instrumental music at carnival time in Trinidad was originally provided by African drums, but these were banned in 1884, after which the resourceful Trinidadians developed the *tamboo-bamboo* band – instruments made of hollowed-out bamboo that could be tuned to different notes. The word *tamboo* is a local dialect version of the French *tambour* (a small drum) but these 'drums' were relatively quiet and in the 1930s they were supplemented (and soon replaced) by the sound of metallic percussion in the form of homemade instruments fashioned from anything to hand that would make a noise, such as dustbin lids and car brake-drums.

One of these, called the ping pong, was made from a large paint tin and struck with wooden sticks. The beaters left indentations and it was discovered that if these were pushed out to form small bumps, they could be tuned to notes of different pitch. During the second world war the Americans used Trinidad as an army base, leaving behind vast quantities of big empty oildrums. The principle of the ping pong was extended to these much larger containers, which quickly proved to be very versatile instruments.

The oildrum is turned upside down and its base hammered into a concave curve. Individual notes are then grooved with a steel punch. There may be only three or four separate notes on bass instruments but as many as 29 on a soprano pan. The steel is tempered by heating and then cooled rapidly in water to give a better tone. The height of the drum is reduced as needed to give the optimum resonance for its range and its notes are then fine-tuned. Smaller steel pans are suspended by wire from a stand, but bass pans usually consist of entire oildrums that stand on the ground. They are played with sticks made of bamboo or other wood that have bands of rubber wound around the ends (or sponge rubber balls for bass pans).

Steel-pan playing was originally an aural tradition in which the players would work out their parts, or be shown what to play by the leader, and would then memorise it. NAM 60 is a transcription of the recording and does not reflect all the detail of the performance.

Steel pans

The size of a steel band can vary from just a quartet to a huge ensemble of 100 or more players. Although the names given to the various sizes of pan varies between ensembles and regions, their musical functions are usually similar:

Name	Musical function
Soprano, Tenor, First tenor, Ping pong	Melody-line pans, with a chromatic range of at least two octaves
Double alto, Double second, Double tenor	A pair of pans that can play an alto melody line or chords
Cello, Guitar, Triple cello, Four-pan cello	Sets of two, three or four pans that can play a tenor part or chords
Bass, Boom	Bass line (usually a set of five or six pans, each with three or four notes)

The smaller pans usually have a fully chromatic range of two and a half octaves. The 12 lowest semitones are arranged in a **circle of 5ths**, forming the outer circle of notes (shown *left*, looking down from above). Inside this is a second (higher) octave of notes, and the remaining four or five notes, which are an octave higher still, are in the middle of the pan. Tuning adjacent notes in 5ths and octaves like this improves the resonance of the instrument.

Traditional steel bands once included a section called 'the iron' – several people playing rhythms with metal rods on brake drums from old cars. Today, it is more common for a steel band to include a drum kit (which you probably heard in the recording of NAM 60, although its part is not included in the score). There may also be a pair of conga drums, and some steel bands include other metallic percussion instruments such as the vibraphone.

Yellow Bird became a popular addition to traditional steel-band repertory, because of its memorable melody, simple harmonies and clearly defined structures. Modern steel-band playing has widened this repertoire considerably, with special arrangements of many different types of music.

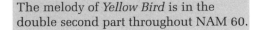

The melody of *Yellow Bird* is in the double second part throughout NAM 60.

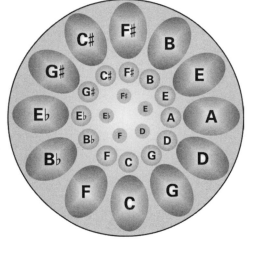

Commentary

The piece starts with the chorus of the song, which falls into four four-bar phrases that form a **binary** structure:

    A bars 1–4
    A bars 5–8
    B bars 9–12
    B¹ bars 13–16

Notice the use of both melodic sequence (bars 9–10) and varied repetition (compare bar 11 with bar 10). These 16 bars are played twice, as indicated by the repeat mark at the end of bar 16.

The verse of the song then follows, which has just two phrases (bars 17–20 and 21–25). The second of these phrases at last breaks the **periodic phrasing** by including an extra bar of V⁷ harmony (bar 24).

The whole of these 25 bars are then repeated to form the rest of the piece. Notice the harmony part that briefly rises above the tune in bars 28–29 and 32–33 to give this repeat a little variety.

Each part has its own clearly-defined function, which is maintained throughout the arrangement. The basses play chordal notes in a tango rhythm that never varies. The four-pan cello is a simple harmony part that moves in semibreves and minims. The double tenor plays a counter-rhythm in the first seven bars of the A sections adding 6ths to the tonic chords and 7ths to the dominant chords, but it is confined to semibreves elsewhere. The melody is assigned to the upper instruments throughout, and is doubled in 3rds during the approach to the perfect cadence that ends every main section of the piece.

The melody is largely diatonic (C♯ is the only chromatic note) and its limited range (from D above middle C to E a 9th higher) reveals its origins as a song. Notice how the long notes are sustained by the use of a **tremolo** (or roll) on the pans.

We have already noted that the harmonisation uses only three chords (G, D⁷ and C). There is no modulation, but the secondary dominant (G7) created by the passing F♮ in bar 8 and similar places adds a touch of chromaticism to the otherwise diatonic harmony. The texture is **homophonic** throughout the entire piece.

Exercise 12

1.   What is meant by syncopation?

2.   Give the number of the first bar in which there is no syncopation in any printed part.

3.   What do you notice about the part played by the four-pan cello?

4.   In bars 1–8 the melody is mainly stepwise. On what is the melody of the next six bars based?

5.   What is meant by the term tremolo?

6.   Briefly describe the tonality and texture of *Yellow Bird*.

Sample questions

In Section B of the Unit 6 paper there will be three questions on pieces from the Applied Music area of study, of which you will have to answer two. Here are three to use for practice.

You can write in continuous prose or short note form. You will be allowed to refer to an unmarked copy of NAM, and you should give the location of each specific feature that you mention. Aim to complete each question in 20 minutes.

(a) Which features, apart from the text, of *O Wilhelme, pastor bone* by John Taverner (NAM 26, pages 266–269), indicate that it is a piece of church music dating from the Renaissance?

(b) How does James Horner use music to convey the grandeur of Titanic's maiden voyage, as well as a sense of Irish emigrants setting sail for a new life, in the score of *Titanic* (1997): 'Take her to sea, Mr Murdoch' (NAM 47, pages 440–460).

(c) Show how features of both Caribbean and European music are blended in *Yellow Bird* (NAM 60, pages 528–529).

Glossary

Not all of the terms in this glossary will be relevant to the set works that you are studying.

A cappella. Italian for 'in church style'. A term that refers to unaccompanied singing (as in NAM 26).

Accented passing note. A dissonant note sounded on the beat and filling the gap between two harmony notes. In NAM 1 the note B in the first violin part at the start of bar 82 is an accented passing note, clashing with the underlying chord of C. *See also* **Appoggiatura** and **Passing note**.

Aeolian mode. *See* **Modes**.

Anacrusis. One or more weak-beat notes before the first strong beat of a phrase, as at the start of NAM 49. Often called a 'pick-up' in jazz and pop music.

Anticipation. A note played immediately before the chord to which it belongs. The anticipated note is often the tonic in a perfect cadence, as in bar 426 of NAM 1, where the semiquaver G at the end of the bar anticipates the tonic in the final chord of the movement.

Antiphony. The alternation of different groups of instruments and/or singers. NAM 14 begins with an antiphonal texture involving two groups of instruments. Shorter antiphonal exchanges occur in bars 31–39 of the same work.

Appoggiatura. A dissonant non-chord note, often approached by a leap, that resolves by moving to a chord note. In NAM 4 the B played by the violins at the start of bar 17 is an appoggiatura that clashes with the chord of F played by the rest of the orchestra. It then resolves by falling to the chord note A in the second half of the same bar.

Arco. An instruction for string players to resume bowing after using some other technique, such as **pizzicato**, as seen in NAM 4 (lower strings, bar 17).

Aria. Italian for a song, but used mainly to describe an extended vocal solo in opera and church music of the Baroque and Classical periods. The fourth movement of NAM 28 is called an obbligato aria because it includes an obligatory instrumental solo which is heard in counterpoint with the voice.

Articulation. The degree of separation between notes. In NAM 23 the slurs in the first piece indicate that it should be articulated smoothly (legato). Most of the notes in the second piece are marked with staccato dots, indicating a detached style of articulation. At the start of the third piece, the combination of slurs and staccato dots indicates mezzo-staccato – notes that should be only slightly detached.

Atonal. Western music without a note that acts as a home pitch to which all other notes are related. This means, in particular, that atonal music avoids major and minor keys (and also **modes**). NAM 8 is atonal.

Augmentation. A proportionate increase in the note-lengths of a melody. In the second violin part of NAM 18, the crotchets in the upper part of bars 105^1–107 are a doubly augmented version of the semiquavers in bar 101 of the same part.

Augmented-6th chord. A chromatic chord based on the sixth degree of the scale (the flattened sixth degree if the key is major) and the note an augmented 6th above it. The chord also contains a major 3rd above the root and may include a perfect 5th or augmented 4th above the root. An augmented-6th chord can be seen in bar 7 of NAM 17, where the key is E♭ major and the augmented 6th is formed by the notes C♭ and A♮. The chord resolves when the two notes forming the augmented 6th move outward by a semitone to the dominant, as occurs on the first beat of the next bar.

Auxiliary note. A non-chord note that is a step above or below two harmony notes of the same pitch. In bar 39 of NAM 1 the A in the first flute part is a lower auxiliary and the first C is an upper auxiliary. In both cases the harmony note is B.

Balanced phrasing. *See* **Periodic phrasing**.

Baroque. A term referring to music written in styles typical of the period 1600–1750, such as NAM 1.

Bend. *See* **Pitch bend**.

Binary form. A two-part musical structure in which both sections are usually repeated. The first 16 bars of NAM 60 form a binary structure which could be represented by the letters AABB[1]. *See also* **Rounded binary form**.

Blue note. A term used in jazz and blues-based music for a note (usually the third, fifth or seventh degree of a major scale) that is made expressive by slightly lowering its pitch. In the vocal part of NAM 50 the D♭ at the end of bar H2 is the blue 7th of E♭ major and the G♭ in bar H6 is the blue 3rd.

Break. An instrumental solo in pop or jazz, as in the two bars before the first chorus of NAM 50.

Cadence. The last notes or chords of a phrase, suggesting a point of repose. *See* **Perfect cadence**, **Imperfect cadence**, **Interrupted cadence**, **Plagal cadence** and **Phrygian cadence**.

Cadential $\frac{6}{4}$. A **triad** in second inversion is called a $\frac{6}{4}$ chord because its upper notes form intervals of a 6th and a 4th above its bass note. A cadential $\frac{6}{4}$ refers to chord Ic used before a perfect cadence (Ic–V$^{(7)}$–I) or as the first chord of an imperfect cadence (Ic–V). It is one of the most characteristic sounds of the Classical style and can be found in NAM 17, where a perfect cadence in B♭ major is formed by the progression Ic–V^7–I in bars 97–98.

Canon. Music in which a melody in one part fits with the same melody in another part even though the latter starts a few beats later. The device occurs in the type of song known as a round. In the first movement of NAM 28, the melody played by the trumpet is played in canon a 4th lower by two oboes in **unison**. *See also* **Counterpoint**.

Cantus firmus. A pre-existing melody used as the basis of a contrapuntal piece, such as the **chorale** melody played in **canon** by the wind instruments in the first movement of NAM 28.

Chamber music. Ensemble music intended for only one performer per part, such as NAM 16. The term originally referred to music that was suitable to be played in a room (or chamber) of a private house.

Changes. In jazz, a chord **progression** used as the basis for improvisation. The changes in NAM 49 are based on the 12-bar blues. *See also* **Head**.

Chorale. A German hymn melody, such as the one played in **canon** by the wind instruments in the opening chorus of NAM 28. The term is also used for four-part harmonisations of such melodies by composers such as Bach, as seen in the third movement of NAM 28.

Chorus (1). In jazz, a complete unit of music that is restated a number of times in succession, each time with improvised variations. The start of each chorus is marked in the score of NAM 50.

Chorus (2). *See* **Verse-and-chorus form**.

Chromatic. A word meaning 'coloured', used to describe notes outside the current key or mode. They are added for colour and do not cause a change of key. The C♯ and B♭ in bars 1 and 3 of the first piece in NAM 23 are chromatic and do not alter the key of the music, which the perfect cadences in bars 7–8 and 21–22 confirm to be G major. *See also* **Tonality**.

Circle of 5ths. A series of chords whose roots fall in 5ths. Because the roots would soon drop below the lowest note available on most instruments, the bass usually alternates between falling a 5th and rising a 4th, producing the same series of pitches. NAM 14 contains part of a circle of 5ths in bars 36–41.

Classical. A term often used for any sort of art music, but more specifically referring to music written in styles typical of the period 1750–1825, such as NAM 16, 17 and 29.

Coda. The final section of a movement. In tonal music the coda will often consist of material confirming the tonic key. For example, the coda of NAM 17 (bars 233–288) reinforces E♭ major as the home key through tonic and dominant pedals as well as repeated perfect cadences in E♭ major during the last 14 bars.

Codetta. A little coda. The final section of part of a movement. In NAM 17, bars 98^3–111 form a codetta to reinforce the dominant key at the end of this first section of the movement.

Colotomic. A structure found in gamelan music (such as NAM 59) in which nested patterns of beats are terminated by different types of sound. For example, a small gong might be struck after every four beats, a larger one after every eight beats and the largest of all after a cycle of 16 beats.

Comping. A term derived from 'accompanying' and used in jazz for a mainly improvised, chordal style of accompaniment as heard in the piano part of NAM 50.

Concertino. *See* **Concerto grosso**.

Concerto grosso. A type of instrumental music in several movements that was popular in the late Baroque period and which features a group of soloists (called the **concertino**) who share musical material with a larger group (called the **ripieno**). NAM 1 is the first movement of such a concerto.

Concord. *See* **consonance**.

Conjunct. Movement to an adjacent note (a tone or a semitone away) in a melody, also known as stepwise motion. In the first 12 bars of NAM 13 the top part is entirely conjunct. The opposite of conjunct is **disjunct**.

Consonance. An harmonious sound or concord, lacking tension. The opposite of **dissonance**.

Continuo. Abbreviation of *basso continuo*. A continuous bass part of the Baroque period played on one or more bass instruments. It also provides the foundation for improvising harmonies on chordal instruments such as the harpsichord, organ and lute. Such improviation was done in accordance with the conventions of the time, guided by any **figured bass** given in the part (see NAM 28). The term is also used to mean the instrumental group that plays the continuo part.

Contrapuntal. Adjectival form of **counterpoint**.

Contrary motion. Simultaneous melodic lines that move in opposite directions. In the first piece in NAM 23, the melody and bass move in contrary motion during the first six bars – when the melody rises, the bass falls, and vice versa. *See also* **Oblique motion**, **Parallel motion** and **Similar motion**.

Cori spezzati. Italian for 'divided choirs'. A term used to describe the spatially separated groups of performers in **polychoral** music such as NAM 14 and NAM 27.

Countermelody. A melody of secondary importance heard at the same time as (and therefore in **counterpoint** with) a more important melody. In NAM 17 the horn melody in bars 250–253 is combined with a cello countermelody.

Counterpoint. The simultaneous combination of two or more melodies that usually have independent rhythms. There may be **imitation** between the parts but counterpoint can also be non-imitative. A whole movement may be contrapuntal or a piece might alternate between contrapuntal and other textures, as in NAM 18, where a section of fugal counterpoint begins at bar 67. The term counterpoint is often used interchangeably with **polyphony**.

Countersubject. *See* **Fugue**.

Cross-rhythm. A passage in which the rhythmic patterns of one or more parts runs counter to the normal accentuation or grouping of notes in the prevailing metre. In NAM 18, the triplet quavers in bars 226–241 (left-hand piano part, then cello) create a cross-rhythm against the normal quavers in the other parts.

Development. The central section of **sonata form**. The term is also used more generally to describe the manipulation and transformation of motifs and themes in any sort of music.

Dialogue. A texture in which motifs pass between different parts. In bars 148–151 of NAM 17, there is a dialogue between the cello (playing a four-note motif that ends with a fall of an octave) and the viola and woodwind in octaves (which play a similar motif that ends with a rising 3rd).

Diatonic. Music which contains only the pitches of the prevailing key or mode, with no chromatic notes. NAM 12 is diatonic throughout.

Diminished-7th chord. A four-note chord made up of superimposed minor 3rds (or their **enharmonic** equivalents), creating an interval of a diminished 7th between its outer notes. In the first piece in NAM 23, the notes C♯–E–G–B♭ in the second half of bar 1 form a diminished-7th chord.

Discord. *See* **Dissonance**.

Disjunct. Melodic movement by leaps rather than by steps between adjacent notes, as in NAM 8. The opposite of disjunct is **conjunct**.

Dissonance. Two or more sounds that give the effect of a clash. The clash itself is called a discord. The perception of what sounds dissonant has varied over time. Before the 20th century it was normal for the tension produced by an on-beat discord to be 'resolved' by means of the dissonant note moving to a concordant note. In bar 17 of NAM 4 the violins play a B which is dissonant because it clashes with the chord of F played by the rest of the orchestra. This dissonance then resolves by falling to A (part of the prevailing chord of F major). In earlier music, dissonances were prepared in advance as well as being resolved (*see* **suspension**). However, since about 1900 discords have been freely used with neither preparation nor resolution (most notably in NAM 8).

Dominant preparation. A passage focused on and around the dominant chord to create an expectation that the tonic key will return, as in bars 16–28 of NAM 16, which lead up to a return of the tonic key and opening theme.

Dorian mode. *See* **Modes**.

Double-stopping. The performance of a two-note chord on a string instrument, as occurs in the first-violin part of NAM 16 at bar 41.

Doubling. The assignment of a melody to two or more instruments or voices that perform it together. In NAM 17, the clarinet melody starting at the end of bar 111 is doubled in **unison** by violin, and in octaves by viola, cello and bassoon.

Échappée. A non-chord note that moves by step from a harmony note and then leaps in the opposite direction to another harmony note. The first A♭ in the first-violin part of NAM 16 is an échappée.

Enharmonic. A term to describe the same pitch notated in different ways, such as G♯ and A♭.

Episode. A passage designed to offer a contrast with the main section of a piece, particularly in **rondo form** and **ritornello form**.

Exposition. The first section in **sonata form** or in a **fugue**.

False relation. The occurrence *in different parts* of a note in its normal form and in its chromatically altered form. The two notes may occur simultaneously (e.g. the G♯ minim and G♮ semiquaver on beat 3 of bar 96 in NAM 20) or they may occur in close proximity (e.g. the G♯ and G♮ between the outer parts in bar 13 of the pavane in NAM 13).

Figure. A clearly-defined melodic fragment such as the six notes heard in the ripieno first-violin part in bars 14–15 of NAM 1. This is repeated in sequence in the next six bars. When a figure such as this is repeated exactly, varied, or used in sequence the result is called figuration. *See also* **Motif**.

Figured bass. Numbers and other symbols below a **continuo** part to indicate the harmonies to be improvised by chordal instruments, as in NAM 28.

Fill. A term used in jazz and pop music for a brief improvised flourish (often on drums) to fill the gap between one section of a piece and the next.

Fugal. A texture that has some of the features of a **fugue**, without having the structure of a complete fugue. The Italian word *fugato* is often used for a fugal section within a longer movement (as in bars 67–100 of NAM 18 and bars 22–61 of NAM 29).

Fugue. A type of composition based on a melody that initially enters in succession in each of several parts. This is called the subject (or the answer if it is transposed). While each subsequent part introduces the subject, the previous part continues with a new idea called the countersubject that fits in **counterpoint** with the subject. The first part of a fugue, known as the **exposition**, ends after each

part has introduced the subject or answer. There is no set pattern for the rest of a fugue, but there will generally be further entries of the subject, often in related keys, and towards the end there may be a **stretto**.

Functional harmony. Progressions of chords, particularly $V^{(7)}$–I, that define the key(s) of a piece of music. In NAM 1, the progression I–V–I is heard four times in the first 12 bars, firmly establishing G major as the tonic key.

Genre (pronounced jon-ruh). A category or type of composition, such as the piano sonata, the string quartet or the madrigal.

Glissando. A slide between two different pitches. On an instrument such as the harp, a finger is run across the strings so that a fast succession of pitches is heard. On instruments such as the violin and trombone, and when singing, it is possible to glide smoothly from one pitch to another so that the intervening pitches are not heard as separate notes. Singers and string players often refer to this effect as portamento.

Harmonic. On string instruments (including the harp and guitar), a very high and pure sound produced by placing a finger lightly on a string before plucking or bowing. Harmonics are indicated by small circles above the harp notes in bars 108–109 of NAM 5.

Harmonic rhythm. The rate at which chords change. There are two chords (I and V^7) in bar 1 of NAM 16, but in bars 9–12 the harmonic rhythm is much slower – chord V and chord I both last for two bars.

Head arrangement. A jazz arrangement worked out in rehearsal and then memorised ('in the head'). It starts with a section called the head, which may include a composed theme, and which introduces a chord progression known as the **changes**. After this the changes are repeated a number of times, above which each principal player improvises variations. Each repetition of the changes is called a **chorus**. The head may be repeated at the end of the performance, in which case it is called the 'out chorus'. NAM 50 is a head arrangement.

Hemiola. A rhythmic device in which two groups of three beats ('strong–weak–weak, strong–weak–weak') are articulated as three groups of two beats ('strong–weak, strong–weak, strong–weak'). See the example printed on page 82.

Heterophony. A texture in which simple and elaborated versions of the same melody are heard together, as in bars 9–14 of NAM 29, where the violins play a decorated version of the soprano melody.

Hexatonic. Music based on a scale of six pitches. The first 26 bars of NAM 12 are based on the six notes B, C♯, E, F♯, G♯ and A♯. *See also* **Pentatonic**.

Homophonic. A musical texture in which one part (usually the uppermost) has the melodic interest and the other parts accompany (as opposed to a polyphonic or contrapuntal texture, in which all the parts are melodically interesting). Bars 78–87 of NAM 43 are homophonic; since they consist entirely of block chords, they could also be described as **homorhythmic** or chordal. NAM 60 illustrates a different type of homophony, often referred to as 'melody-dominated homophony' or, more simply, 'melody and accompaniment'.

Homorhythmic. A type of **homophonic** texture in which all of the parts move in the same rhythm, such as in bars 78–87 of NAM 43.

Imitation. A **contrapuntal** device in which a melody in one part is copied a few notes later in a different part (and often at a different pitch) while the melody in the first part continues. The imitation is usually not exact – some intervals may be modified, but the basic melodic shape and rhythm of the opening should be clear. In bar 24 of NAM 29, tenors enter in imitation of the basses, and imitative entries in the alto and soprano parts then follow. If parts continue in *exact* imitation for a number of bars, they form a **canon**.

Imperfect cadence. Two chords at the end of a phrase, the second of which is the dominant, as in NAM 23, No. 11, bars 4 and 8. *See also* **Phrygian cadence**.

Impressionism. A style particularly associated with late 19th- and early 20th-century French music. Just as Impressionist painters would blur objects and explore the effects of light, so Impressionist composers would blur tonality and explore the effects of unusual and delicate tone colours, often using chords more for their sound qualities than for the purpose of defining keys. NAM 5 is typical of the Impressionist style in music.

Interrupted cadence. Two chords at the end of a phrase, the first of which is the dominant and the second being any chord *other than* the dominant or tonic (most often chord VI, as in bar 26 of the third

piece in NAM 23, where the cadence is V⁷–VI in the key of E minor).

Inversion (1). An interval is inverted when its lower note is transposed up an octave while the other note remains the same (or vice versa).

Inversion (2). A chord is inverted when a note other than the root of the chord is sounding in the bass. NAM 17 begins with a chord of E♭ major in root position, followed in bar 3 by E♭ major in first inversion (i.e. with its third, G, in the bass).

Inversion (3). A melody is inverted when every interval is kept the same but now moves in the opposite direction (e.g. a rising 3rd followed by a falling 4th when inverted becomes a falling 3rd following by a rising 4th).

Klangfarbenmelodie. A German term for a melody in which the instrumental timbre is constantly changing, as in NAM 8. *See also* **Pointillism**.

Leitmotif. A musical idea, particularly in German opera of the Romantic period (such as NAM 4) representing an object, emotion or person.

Lydian mode. *See* **Modes**.

Melisma. Several notes sung to one syllable. In the first bar of NAM 29 the word-setting is **syllabic**, but at the start of bar 2 the first syllable of 'solus' is set to a short melisma.

Melody-dominated homophony. *See* **Homophonic**.

Metre. The organisation of a regular pulse into patterns of strong and weak beats. For example, alternate strong and weak beats are known as duple metre, while the recurring pattern 'strong–weak–weak' is known as triple metre.

Minimalism. A musical style of the late 20th century characterised by static or slowly changing harmonies and the interaction of short patterns that repeat and change over a considerable length of time, as in NAM 12. *See also* **Postmodernism**.

Mirror canon. A **canon** in which the imitative part is an **inversion** of the main part. The technique has been used by composers such as Bach and Mozart, but it is particularly associated with such **serial music** as NAM 8.

Modal. Relating to the use of one or more **modes** in music.

Modernism. A term used to describe styles of the 20th-century century that are experimental and/or atonal, such as NAM 8. *See also* **Postmodernism**.

Modes. These are usually taken to mean seven-note scales apart from modern major and minor scales (although some people refer to these as the major mode and minor mode). The aeolian mode starting on A consists of the notes A–B–C–D–E–F–G–A. It differs from A minor in having G♮ rather than G♯ as its seventh degree. The dorian mode starting on D consists of the notes D–E–F–G–A–B–C–D and the lydian mode starting on F consists of the notes F–G–A–B–C–D–E–F. All of these modes can be transposed to start on any note, in which case the order of tones and semitones between the notes remains the same. For example, the dorian mode on E is E–F♯–G–A–B–C♯–D–E.

Modulation. The process by which music changes from one key to another. NAM 1 begins in the key of G major. The introduction of C♯s from bar 15 onwards indicates the start of a modulation to the dominant key of D major. This new key is then confirmed by a succession of I–V–I progressions in D major, starting in bar 23.

Monophonic. A texture that consists of a single unaccompanied melody, as at the start of NAM 43.

Monothematic. A movement in which the melodic material derives from a single theme, such as NAM 16.

Motif. A short but memorable melodic fragment that is subject to manipulation through techniques such as sequence, inversion or extension. The motivic material in the first two bars of NAM 16 forms the basis of almost all the thematic material in the entire movement. See also **Figure**.

Neapolitan 6th. The first inversion of the triad on the flattened second degree of a scale. In the key of E minor, this is a chord of F major in first inversion, as on the first beat of bar 155 in NAM 1.

Neoclassical. An early 20th-century style that combines forms and techniques from the 18th century with a more modern approach to elements such as rhythm, harmony and instrumentation. NAM 19 shows the influence of Neoclassicism.

Obbligato aria. See **Aria**.

Oblique motion. The relationship between a melodic part that remains on a single pitch with another part that simultaneously either moves away from it (as at the start of the third piece in NAM 23, where the melody remains on B while the bass moves down chromatically) or towards it. See also **Contrary motion**, **Parallel motion** and **Similar motion**.

Ostinato. A melodic, rhythmic or chordal pattern repeated throughout a substantial passage of music, such as the two-bar timpani pattern starting at bar 40 in NAM 43. In popular music and jazz a melodic ostinato is known as a riff.

Parallel major and parallel minor. Keys that share the same tonic, such as C major and C minor are known as parallel keys. The two keys can also be described as the tonic major and tonic minor. The main key of NAM 18 is C minor, but the trio (bars 193^2–261) is in the parallel major (C major).

Parallel motion. A type of similar motion in which the parts move in the same direction and maintain the same or similar vertical intervals between notes. A succession of similar intervals can be described as being in parallel (e.g. the parallel 3rds between flutes in bars 3–6 of NAM 1), as can a succession of similar chords that have the same spacing (e.g. the parallel 7th chords in bars 35–41 of NAM 24). See also **Contrary motion**, **Oblique motion** and **Similar motion**.

Passing note. A non-chord note that most commonly fills the gap between two harmony notes a 3rd apart. In the third bar of NAM 1 the second quaver in both flute parts is a passing note between harmony notes belonging to the chord of G major. See also **Accented passing note**.

Pedal (or 'pedal point'). A sustained or repeated note against which changing harmonies are heard. A pedal on the dominant (NAM 16, bars 16–28) tends to create excitement and the feeling that the tension must be resolved by a move to the tonic. A pedal on the tonic anchors the music to its key note (NAM 16, bars 107–111^1). If a pedal occurs in the uppermost part, rather than the bass, it is called an inverted pedal (NAM 16, bars 111^2–115).

Pentatonic. Music based on a scale of five pitches. You can find one such scale by playing the five black notes on a keyboard instrument. NAM 59 is pentatonic, although the five pitches used are not identical to those found in most western scales. See also **Hexatonic**.

Perfect cadence. Chords V and I at the end of a phrase, as in the last two chords of NAM 13.

Periodic phrasing. Balanced phrases of regular lengths (usually two, four or eight bars) – a style particularly associated with music of the Classical period. See the music example on page 40.

Phasing. A technique used in some minimalist music, in which repeating patterns gradually move between being in phase (when their rhythms coincide) and out of phase (when their rhythms do not coincide). See the example on page 59.

Phrygian cadence. A type of **imperfect cadence** used in minor keys, particularly in the Renaissance and Baroque periods. It consists of the specific progression IVb–V, as in bars 15^2–16 of the galliard in NAM 13.

Pick-up. *See* **Anacrusis**.

Pitch bend. A term used in pop and jazz for an expressive short slide in pitch to or from a note, particularly a blue note. In NAM 49 pitch bends are indicated by diagonal lines in bars 3 and 7.

Pizzicato (pizz.) An instruction to a player of a bowed string instrument to pluck the strings instead of bowing them, as seen in the parts for lower strings at bar 16 in NAM 4. *See also* **Arco**.

Plagal cadence. Chord IV followed by chord I at the end of a phrase, as in bars 79–80 of NAM 14.

Pointillism. A 20th-century style in which the texture of the music is made up of individual points of sound, as in NAM 8.

Polarised texture. A term referring to Baroque music in which there is a wide gap between the bass part and the melody line(s), as in in bars 4–6 of NAM 1. In performance, this gap is normally filled by improvised chords played on a continuo instrument such as an organ, harpsichord or lute.

Polychoral. Music intended for at least two groups of performers who are usually placed in separate parts of a building. Polychoral music was developed at St Mark's, Venice, in the late Renaissance and was popular until the early years of the Baroque period. NAM 14 and NAM 27 contain examples of the style. *See also* **Cori spezzati**.

Polyphony. The simultaneous use of two or more melodies. The first 32 bars of NAM 26 are polyphonic. Nowadays, the term is often used interchangeably with counterpoint, although it is more common to use polyphony when referring to vocal music of the Renaissance period.

Portamento. See Glissando.

Postmodernism. Musical styles of the late 20th and early 21st centuries that have features such as familiar scales and modes, and that often avoid extreme dissonance, unlike the earlier **atonal** styles of **modernism**. Many people regard **minimalism** (typified by NAM 12) as a type of postmodernism.

Prime order. *See* **Tone row**.

Progression. A series of chords designed to follow one another.

Quartal harmony. Chords built from superimposed 4ths, rather than on 3rds as they are in triads. The use of quartal harmony can be seen in bars 23–28 of NAM 24.

Recapitulation. *See* **Sonata form**.

Recitative. A type of music for one or more solo voices that usually has minimal accompaniment and in which the object is to convey the words in a style approaching the natural rhythms of speech, rather than to create the formal melodies of song. Recitative was common in opera and church music of the Baroque and Classical periods. The second movement of NAM 28 is a recitative.

Refrain. A passage of music that returns at intervals throughout a work, especially in **rondo form**, although the term is also used to refer to the chorus of a song in **verse-and-chorus form**.

Register. A specific part of the range of a voice or instrument. For example, the first-violin part in NAM 18 starts in a low register, but climbs to a high register in bars 135–137.

Renaissance. A term referring to music written in styles typical of the period 1400–1600, such as NAM 26 (dating from about 1528).

Resultant melody. When several different parts of similar **timbre** are heard simultaneously, the highest (or loudest) notes may seem to form a new part, known as a resultant melody. Such melodies are found in some types of world music and in **minimalism** (e.g. the live clarinet part in bars 25–26 of NAM 12 is a resultant melody derived from the parts for clarinets 1–3).

Retrograde. Moving backwards. A process in which a new melody is formed by playing the pitches of a previous melody in reverse order. Used in serial music (such as NAM 8) and in styles based on **serialism** (such as NAM 44). If the intervals of the original melody are inverted in addition to the pitches being played in reverse order, the result is known as retrograde inversion.

Retrograde inversion. *See* **Retrograde**.

Riff. *See* **Ostinato**.

Rim shot. In pop and jazz, an accented note produced by striking the rim and the head of a snare drum simultaneously, or by positioning one stick with its tip on the drum head and its shaft on the rim, and then striking it with another stick.

Ripieno. *See* **Concerto grosso**.

Ritornello form. A structure used for large-scale movements of the late-Baroque period, such as NAM 1. An opening instrumental section (called the ritornello) introduces the main musical ideas. It is followed by a contrasting texture, although usually based on similar material, that features one or more soloists. Sections of the ritornello, often in different keys, then alternate with solo textures until the complete ritornello (or most of it) returns in the tonic key at the end of the movement. The fragmentary nature of most of the ritornello sections gives the form its name – ritornello means a 'little return'.

Romantic. A term referring to music written in styles typical of the 19th and early 20th centuries, such as NAM 4, 18 and 23.

Rondo form. A musical structure in which a refrain in the tonic key alternates with contrasting episodes, creating a pattern such as ABACA or ABACABA. NAM 16 is a rondo.

Rounded binary form. A type of **binary form** in which material from the opening returns towards the end of the second section, transposed to the tonic key if necessary. This structure, which could be represented as ‖:A:‖:BA:‖, is used in the first two pieces of NAM 23. Unlike **ternary form** (ABA), the B section in rounded binary form usually does *not* provide a clear contrast with the A section. Neither is it a self-contained section, because the B section in rounded binary leads straight back to a repeat (or an abbreviated repeat) of the A section.

Rubato. A term meaning 'robbed' that refers to shortening some beats and lengthening others when perfroming, in order to give an expressive, free feel to the pulse. The use of rubato is particularly associated with piano music of the Romantic period, such as NAM 23.

Secondary dominant. A chord (with or without a 7th) used as the dominant of a major or minor *triad* (other than I) rather than as the dominant of a key. In NAM 49, the C^7 in bar 54, is a secondary dominant because it is the dominant of the chord that follows. There is no modulation to F major because E♭ appears almost immediately, turning the second chord into F^7 and thus making it another secondary dominant (of the chord of B♭^{7} in bar 55).

Sequence. The *immediate* repetition at a different pitch of a motif, phrase or chord progression. A series of such repetitions is frequently used in the spinning-out of Baroque melodic lines, as in bars 69–75 of NAM 1 (where flutes perform an ascending sequence based on the initial three-note figure). In bars 70–73 this melodic sequence is accompanied by chords that form a harmonic sequence.

Serialism. Music based on manipulations of a chosen order for the 12 degrees of a chromatic scale, as in NAM 8. *See also* **Tone row**.

Similar motion. Melodic lines that move in the same direction at the same time. In bars 93^6–99 of NAM 16 the two violins move in similar motion. *See also* **Contrary motion**, **Oblique motion** and **Parallel motion**.

Sonata form. The most common structure for the first movement (and also often other movements) of sonatas, symphonies, concertos and chamber music in the **Classical** period and later. The essence of sonata form is the use of two contrasting tonal centres (tonic and either the dominant or another closely related key such as the relative major) in a first section called the **exposition**; the use of a wider range of keys to create tension and excitement in a central section called the **development**; and a **recapitulation** in which the music from the exposition is repeated in the tonic key. NAM 17 is a sonata-form movement (preceded by a slow introduction). *See also* **Subject**.

Stepwise movement. *See* **Conjunct**.

Straight quavers (or straight eights). In jazz and pop music, quavers that are played evenly rather than being played as **swing quavers**.

Stretto. The closing up of imitative parts so that they start nearer to each other than they originally did. In NAM 29 each voice part enters in imitation after a gap of two bars from bar 22 until bar 32. But in the stretto of bars 46–48 each of the three upper parts enters after just one bar.

Subject (1). One of the sections in the **exposition** of a movement in **sonata form**. In NAM 17 the first subject of this sonata-form movement begins with the last three quavers of bar 18 and the second subject (in the dominant key) starts at the quaver upbeat to bar 53.

Subject (2). The melodic idea on which a fugue or other type of imitative texture is based, such as the vocal bass part in bars 22–24[1] of NAM 29.

Substitution chord. In jazz, a chord that functions in a similar way to a different chord that it replaces. For example, a jazz musician might play vii$^{\text{dim.7}}$ instead of V^7 as the first chord of a perfect cadence.

Suspension. A device in which a note is first sounded in a consonant context (called the preparation). It is then repeated (or held) over a change of chord so that it becomes a dissonance (this is the suspension itself). Finally, there is a resolution when the suspended note moves by step (usually downwards) to a consonant note. These three stages can be seen in the uppermost part of NAM 13. The note D is prepared over a chord of D in bar 3. It then sounds against the E in the bass of bar 4 (creating the actual suspension). Finally it resolves by falling to C♯ (decorated with a lower **auxiliary note** on B♮), which is part of the chord in the second half bar 4.

Swing quavers (or swung quavers). In jazz and pop music the division of the beat into a pair of notes in which the first is longer than the second. Swing quavers may be notated as ♫ or ♪♫ but they are performed closer to ♩♪ in both cases. There may be an instruction to swing the rhythm at the start of the music (as in NAM 51) or it may be left to the performers' sense of style to know when to play swung rhythms. In NAM 49 triplet signs are used to show an approximation of the swung rhythm, while the instruction 'straight ♪s' ('straight eights') in bar 45 indicates quavers that are played evenly and not swung.

Syllabic. Vocal writing in which all (or most) of the syllables are set to single notes, In the first bar of NAM 29 the word-setting is syllabic, but at the start of bar 2 the first syllable of 'solus' is set to a short **melisma**.

Syncopation. The effect created when notes are used to emphasise unstressed parts of the bar, as in bars 172–179 of NAM 17 where the violin and viola notes fall between beats rather than on beats. Syncopation also occurs when rests rather than notes fall on strong beats, as at the start of NAM 50.

Ternary form. A three-part structure consisting of a middle section flanked by two identical or very similar passages. The form can be represented by the letters ABA or, if there are differences in the A section when it returns, ABA[1]. NAM 18 has a ternary structure, created by the sections Scherzo–Trio–Scherzo. *See also* **Rounded binary form**.

Tertiary shift. A move to an unrelated key that is a 3rd away. Bars 80–84 of NAM 47 are in D major, but a tertiary shift in bar 85 takes the music to the unrelated key of B major at bar 86.

Tessitura. The part of the pitch range in which a passage of music mainly lies. In Bars 242–261 of NAM 18 all instruments are in a low tessitura.

Texture. The relationship between simultaneous layers in a passage of music. *See* **monophonic**, **homophonic**, **homorhythmic**, **polyphony (counterpoint)**, **heterophonic**, **polarised** and **antiphony**.

Theme. A musical idea (usually a melody) that plays an important role in a piece of music.

Through-composed. A piece that avoids creating a structure through the repetition of substantial sections of musical material. NAM 14 could be described as through-composed.

Tierce de Picardie. A major 3rd in the final tonic chord of a passage in a minor key. For example, NAM 20 is in A minor, but the C♯ in bars 15–16 is a tierce de Picardie that turns the tonic triad in these bars into a chord of A *major*.

Timbre (pronounced *tam-bruh*). Tone colour. For example, the clarinet has a different timbre from the trumpet, and it also has different timbres in various parts of its range. The timbre of an instrument can also be affected by the way it is played, for example by using a mute or by plucking a string instead of using the bow.

Tonality. The use of major and minor keys in music and the ways in which these are related to each other. Not all music is tonal – some is modal (based on one or more **modes**) and some (like NAM 59) is based on non-western scales. Western music that uses neither keys nor modes, such as NAM 8, is described as **atonal** (without tonality).

Tone row (or note row). In **serial music**, the order of 12 pitches on which a composition is based. The original order of notes is called the prime order. This can be used backwards (**retrograde** order), or in **inversion** or **retrograde inversion**. All four of these forms of the row can be **transposed** to start on any of the 12 semitones in an octave, giving 48 possible versions of the row in total. NAM 8 is a serial composition based on a note row. *See also* **verticalisation**.

Tonic major and **tonic minor**. *See* **Parallel major** and **Parallel minor**.

Transcription. The notation of music that was previously not written down or that existed in some other type of notation. The scores of popular music, jazz and world music in NAM are all transcriptions from recordings. The term is also used in the sense of 'arrangement' to describe music that has been adapted for different performing resources. In NAM 20, bars 1–16, 33–48 and 82– 98 are free transcriptions of the three eight-bar phrases in NAM 33.

Transposition. The process of writing or performing music at a higher or lower pitch than the original.

Tremolo. The rapid and continuous repetition of a single note, as in the violin and cymbal parts of the last four bars on page 385 of NAM, or the rapid and continuous alternation of two pitches, as in the E♭ clarinet part in the same bars. The same page shows how these two types of tremolo are normally notated. Further examples can be seen in the string parts on page 116 of NAM.

Triad. A three-note chord formed by two super-imposed intervals of a 3rd, such as A–C–E.

Trill. An ornament that consists of rapid alternation of two notes a step apart and that is indicated by the symbol *tr*, as in bar 28 of the bassoon part in NAM 5. The same symbol is also used for a roll on a percussion instrument, even though this doesn't involve different pitches, as can be seen in bars 74–76 of the timpani part in NAM 4.

Tritone. An interval of three tones, such as between C♯ and G, the highest and lowest notes of the flute melody in the first two bars of NAM 5.

Turnaround. In jazz and pop music, a short passage at the end of a section designed to lead the music back to the tonic key for a repeat of an earlier section. This is usually done by ending the turnaround on chord V^7.

Tutti. Italian for 'all' – a term that refers to the full ensemble, or a passage of music intended for the full ensemble. In bar 89 of NAM 1 the word *tutti* signifies the entry of the full orchestra after the violin solo in the previous six bars.

Unison. A term to describe two or more people performing the same note or melody at the same pitch. In bars 55–57 of NAM 44 the first violins play in unison with the flutes. In the clarinet parts of bar 55 'a 2' tells both clarinettists to play in unison.

Verse-and-chorus form. A structure used in many popular songs in which verses (that have similar music but different words) alternate with choruses (in which both the music and the words are usually the same on each appearance). There may also be an introduction at the start, a **coda** at the end, and instrumental sections in the middle to provide variety.

Verticalisation. A technique used in **serial music**, in which adjacent notes of a **tone row** are sounded simultaneously, as occurs in some bars of the piano part of NAM 8.

Vibrato. Small but fast fluctuations in the pitch of a note to add warmth and expression. The technique is not possible on instruments that produce notes of fixed pitch, such as the piano or harp, but is used by most other instrumentalists and trained singers. The speed and width of vibrato depends on the context and style – in Baroque times, vibrato was regarded as a type of ornament to be used with discretion, while in Romantic music it was used relatively frequently. The saxophone solo in NAM 49 shows how a wide vibrato was a standard technique in early jazz.

Virtuoso. A performer of great technical skill. The term is also used to describe music which requires a high level of technical skill.

Vocalising. Singing to vowel sounds rather than real words, as in the choral parts of NAM 47.

Walking bass. A bass part that maintains the same note-lengths throughout a substantial passage of music. The term is mainly used in pop and jazz – for example, NAM 49 starts with a walking bass, and another example occurs starts in bar 1.1 of NAM 50.

Whole-tone scale. A scale in which there is a whole tone between every adjacent note. It occurs in the clarinet and flute solos in bars 32–33 of NAM 5.

For further help on technical terminology, consult the *Rhinegold Dictionary of Music in Sound* by David Bowman. It provides detailed explanations of a wide range of musical concepts and illustrates them using a large number of specially recorded examples on its accompanying compact discs. The *Rhinegold Dictionary of Music in Sound* is published by Rhinegold Publishing, ISBN 978-0946890-87-3.

Elements of Music

When answering the questions for Unit 6, aim to show that you can use music terminology correctly. The following lists may help to remind you of some of the matters to discuss when writing about the features of a particular piece of music. It is not possible to include every point that could arise and some terms *below* may not be relevant to the particular set works you have studied. However, most of these terms can be looked up in the glossary on the preceding pages.

Some of the points *below* are relevant to more than one element of music. For example, cadences might be discussed under harmony, but they also help to define the tonality of music and they often mark off sections in the structure of a piece. When answering exam questions, remember to illustrate your points by referring to specific examples in NAM, citing the bar and beat numbers, and the name of the part in which a feature occurs, as appropriate.

Structure

Binary form
Rounded binary form
Ternary form
Rondo form
Ritornello form
Sonata form (Exposition, Development and
    Recapitulation)

Head arrangement
Verse-and-chorus form
Colotomic structure
Through-composed composition

Introduction
Interlude
Episode
Fugato (and stretto)
Codetta
Coda

Phrase structure
    Use of motifs and cadence points
    Periodic phrasing
Monothematic structure

Melody

Conjunct (scalic or stepwise)
Disjunct (based on leaps, perhaps triadic)
Characteristic intervals (e.g. 3rds)
Rising, falling or arch-shaped melody
Monotone (single pitch)

Motifs
Leitmotifs
Note rows

Phrase structure (balanced or irregular)
    Long phrases or fragmented ideas?

Ornaments and melodic decoration (passing notes,
    auxiliaries, anticipations, etc.)
Blue notes and/or pitch bend

Tonality

Major
Minor
Modal
Chromatic
Atonal (and perhaps also serial)

Pentatonic or hexatonic scales
Cadences to establish tonality

Modulations (to related keys)
Parallel major or parallel minor keys
Tertiary shifts
Unexpected changes of key
Dominant preparation

Texture

Homophonic (melody-dominated homophony)
Homorhythmic
Contrapuntal (or Polyphonic)
    Imitative
    Canonic
    Fugal
    Two-part, three-part, four-part etc.
    Cantus firmus
Monophonic
Heterophonic
Antiphonal
Polarised

Dialogue
Doubling
Phasing
Parallelism (i.e. chains of parallel chords)
The role of rests in the texture

Accompaniment patterns, e.g.:
    Repeated quavers
    Broken chords, arpeggios
    Alberti bass
    Ostinato
    Walking bass

Harmony

Primary triads (I, IV and V)
Root-position chords (and inversions)
Dominant 7ths and Secondary 7ths
Chromatic chords (e.g. Diminished 7th,
    Augmented 6th and Neapolitan 6th)
Functional harmony
Cadences
    Perfect, Imperfect, Plagal, Interrupted
    Phrygian, Modal
Other chord progressions
    Circle of 5ths
    12-bar blues (and other 'changes' in jazz)
Pedal points
Harmonic sequence
Tierce de Picardie
Suspensions and other types of dissonance
Substitution chords

Metre and rhythm

Simple duple metre (e.g. $\frac{2}{8}$, $\frac{2}{4}$ and $\frac{2}{2}$ or $\mathbf{C}$)
Simple triple metre (e.g. $\frac{3}{8}$, $\frac{3}{4}$ and $\frac{3}{2}$)
Simple quadruple metre (e.g. $\frac{4}{8}$, $\frac{4}{4}$ or $\mathbf{C}$, and $\frac{4}{2}$)

Compound duple metre (e.g. $\frac{6}{8}$ and $\frac{6}{4}$)
Compound triple metre (e.g. $\frac{9}{16}$, $\frac{9}{8}$ and $\frac{9}{4}$)
Compound quadruple metre (e.g. $\frac{12}{8}$ and $\frac{12}{4}$)

Irregular metres (e.g. $\frac{5}{8}$, $\frac{7}{8}$, $\frac{5}{4}$ or $\frac{7}{4}$)

Additative rhythms (e.g. 3+3+2 quavers per bar)

Ametric rhythm (no regular pulse)
Polyrhythm (two or more conflicting rhythms)
Cross-rhythm (e.g. 'twos against threes')
Hemiola

Tempo (including changes of speed)
Pause (or *fermata*)
Anacrusis (or pick up)

Syncopation
Ostinato
Augmentation and diminution

On-beat and Off-beat
Down beat (strong beat) and Up beat (weak beat)

Characteristic rhythm patterns, e.g.:
    Triplets
    Dotted rhythms
    Scotch snap (Lombardic rhythm)
    Swung quavers (and straight eights)
    Particular dance rhythms

Resources

Ways in which instruments and/or voices are used
and combined:

Orchestral music
    (large or small orchestra, any solo parts?)
    (natural brass or fully chromatic brass?)
Solo instrumental music
    (e.g. for piano or harpsichord)
Chamber music
    (duet, trio, quartet, etc.)
Continuo instruments in Baroque music

Other types of ensemble, such as gamelan,
    jazz band, jazz combo, rock group etc.

Unusual or electronic instruments
Particular features of writing for instruments
    such as layered textures, pointillist textures,
    contrasting timbres, etc.
Special performance techniques, such as the use of
    mutes, glissando/portamentto, pizzicato, etc.
Is the instrumental writing idiomatic or is it,
    as in NAM 13, suitable for a variety of
    different timbres?

Use of voices:
    Solo and/or choral writing
    Mixed choir, or all male choir – the latter
      perhaps including trebles and countertenors
    Range of voice parts (wide or narrow) and any
      particular tessitura that is used
    Accompanied voices or *a cappella* voices
    Word setting (syllabic or melismatic)
    Vocalising
    Declamatory vocal styles (as in recitative)
    Use of word painting
    Repetition of the text

Miscellaneous

The genre of the work (opera, piano sonata,
    string quartet, symphony, concerto grosso,
    church music, film music etc.)

The original performing circumstances of the
    piece concerned

The role played by dynamics and articulation in
    the music

Parts of the music that are normally improvised
    (including comping and fills in jazz and pop
    music, and the realisation of a figured bass in
    Baroque music).

Index of Works

		Study guide page	Anthology page
NAM 1	*Brandenburg* Concerto No. 4 in G: movement I (Bach)	82	7
NAM 4	Prelude to *Tristan und Isolde* (Wagner)	106	65
NAM 5	*Prélude à L'Après-midi d'un faune* (Debussy)	45	86
NAM 8	Quartet Op. 22: movement I (Webern)	100	160
NAM 12	New York Counterpoint: movement II (Reich)	57	176
NAM 13	Pavane and Galliard (Anthony Holborne)	35	191
NAM 14	*Sonata pian' e forte* (Giovanni Gabrieli)	62	194
NAM 16	String Quartet Op. 33 No. 2 'The Joke': movement IV (Haydn)	38	202
NAM 17	Septet in E♭, Op. 20: movement I (Beethoven)	86	207
NAM 18	Piano Quintet in F minor, Op. 34: movement III (Brahms)	41	231
NAM 19	Sonata for Horn, Trumpet and Trombone: movement I (Poulenc)	49	242
NAM 20	*Pavana Lachrimae* (Sweelinck)	79	245
NAM 23	*Kinderscenen*, Op. 15: Nos. 1, 3 and 11 (Schumann)	89	258
NAM 24	*Pour le piano*: Sarabande (Debussy)	93	260
NAM 26	*O Wilhelme, pastor bone* (Taverner)	109	266
NAM 28	Cantata No. 48, *Ich elender Mensch*: movements I–IV (Bach)	64	288
NAM 29	*Quoniam tu solus* from 'The Nelson Mass' (Haydn)	112	299
NAM 43	*On the Waterfront*: Symphonic Suite (Bernstein)	68	374
NAM 44	*Planet of the Apes*: The Hunt (opening) (Goldsmith)	71	388
NAM 47	*Titanic*: 'Take her to sea, Mr Murdoch' (Horner)	115	440
NAM 49	*Black and Tan Fantasy* (Duke Ellington and Bubber Miley)	96	465
NAM 50	*Four* (opening) (performed by Miles Davis)	52	468
NAM 59	*Baris Melampahan* (traditional Balinese)	76	522
NAM 60	*Yellow Bird* (traditional)	117	528